ART CURRICULUM
ACTIVITIES KITS
Primary Level

Written and illustrated

by

Barbara McNally Reuther

and

Diane Enemark Fogler

PARKER PUBLISHING COMPANY
West Nyack, New York 10995

Printed in the United States of America
10   9   8   7   6   5   4   3   2   1

Library of Congress Cataloging-in-Publication Data

Reuther, Barbara McNally.
   Art curriculum activities kits, primary level.

   1. Art—Study and teaching (Primary)—United States.
2. Activity programs in education—United States.
I. Fogler, Diane Enemark.   II. Title.
N361.R48   1988   372.5'044   87-38483

ISBN 0-13-047142-7

ISBN 0-13-047143-7

PARKER PUBLISHING COMPANY
BUSINESS & PROFESSIONAL DIVISION
A division of Simon & Schuster
West Nyack, New York 10995

About the Authors

Author/illustrator Barbara McNally Reuther, B.A. Art, has taught art at the elementary level for more than seven years in the Rockaway Township School District in New Jersey. Mrs. Reuther has initiated and developed enrichment classes for students gifted in the visual arts and has also worked extensively in the areas of curriculum development and art assessment.

Author Diane Enemark Fogler, M.A. Art, has taught art at the elementary, junior, and senior high school levels for more than twenty years. She currently teaches art at the elementary level and serves as art coordinator for the Rockaway Township School District in New Jersey. Mrs. Fogler has conducted in-service art workshops for classroom teachers and has also worked extensively with gifted students in an art enrichment program. She has served as art director at various day camps and recreation centers and has also written her district's elementary art curriculum as well as several articles for *School Arts Magazine*.

Dedication

To my husband, Charlie,
for his enthusiastic support and encouragement
and to my parents,
the most creative teachers I know.

B.M.R.

To the children I have taught,
who made each day
a challenge and an adventure.

D.E.F.

Acknowledgments

We wish to thank Win Huppuch for the chance he offered us to do this book, and Ann Leuthner for her editorial assistance and reassuring support throughout.

About the Art Curriculum Activities Kits

The *Art Curriculum Activities Kits* will provide teachers with new, stimulating, creative activities that teach basic art concepts and skills and meet the curricular needs of students at various age and skill levels. Within two volumes, the primary and intermediate levels, you will find a comprehensive art curriculum for students in grades 1–8, presented in 150 easy-to-use art lessons. These lessons are carefully designed for the skills sequentially developed between grades 1 and 8. Each lesson has its own full-page illustration and step-by-step student-level directions.

Each book contains three levels, which increase in complexity, and can be used by different grade levels, depending on skill development. Within each level the individual lessons are categorized by the following media: drawing, painting, weaving, color and design, ceramics, paper crafts, printmaking, and crafts. All of the lessons presented make use of inexpensive and commonly available materials and have been classroom tested by the authors and proven to be highly successful.

The organized format and clear graphic presentation of each book make it possible for the teacher with little or no previous art training to teach these lessons successfully. The art specialist will find that these books provide a valuable curricular guide and ability-level source book.

One of the most important features is the skill level sequence. The examples presented below are included to give an overview of the developmental process from Level 1 to Level 6. At each level new skills and media are introduced, while previously acquired skills and techniques are reinforced.

In addition, you'll find detailed, full-page illustrations and easy-to-use directions.

WEAVING

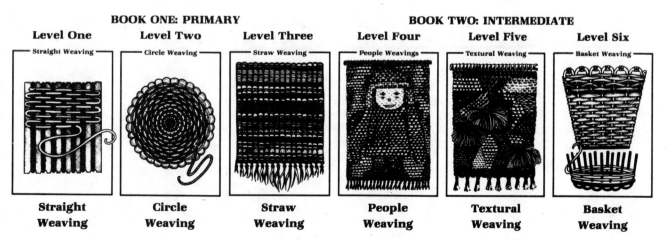

BOOK ONE: PRIMARY			BOOK TWO: INTERMEDIATE		
Level One	**Level Two**	**Level Three**	**Level Four**	**Level Five**	**Level Six**
Straight Weaving	Circle Weaving	Straw Weaving	People Weavings	Textural Weaving	Basket Weaving
Straight Weaving	**Circle Weaving**	**Straw Weaving**	**People Weaving**	**Textural Weaving**	**Basket Weaving**

SPECIAL FEATURES OF THIS BOOK

- A comprehensive, sequential art curriculum designed for beginning levels, or approximately for grades 1–4, depending on individual ability levels.
- Innovative activities in eight different art media which teach basic and advanced art skills and concepts.
- Seventy-five lessons provided with full-page illustrations for each. These illustrations may be used for demonstration purposes or to provide helpful ideas on what to add to each project.
- Smaller "how-to" illustrations are included in the step-by-step directions for ease of use. Direction sheets may also be reproduced and distributed to students for group or independent use.
- Each art concept is built upon another art concept, thus providing a strong foundation for all future art skills.
- Each individual lesson contains a list of materials which makes it easy to see-at-a-glance what is needed for each project.
- Easy-to-use, comprehensive step-by-step directions are provided for each lesson.
- The Table of Contents presents the material in two convenient forms: (1) Activities are categorized by media so that lessons can quickly be found in any given subject area, and (2) media categories are divided into three skill levels so that lessons are easily located for students with varying art skills.
- All of the activities in this book have been classroom tested and proven successful.
- This book explores and introduces a wide variety of art forms and media, which help to build sequential art skills while reinforcing skills previously used. And—each activity is fun and unique—so enjoy!

Contents

About These Kits
Special Features
Focus Areas/Skills Charts

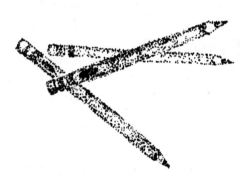

SECTION III

Color and Design

SECTION IV

Ceramics

SECTION VIII   Crafts

Focus Areas

	line	shape	value	color	texture	perspective & proportion	pattern & composition	cultural enrichment	creative thinking
Section I: Drawing									
I-1 Self-Portrait	•	•				•		•	•
I-2 Body Portraits	•	•		•		•		•	•
I-3 Castle Drawings		•				•	•	•	•
I-4 Royal Portrait	•	•		•		•		•	•
I-5 Motivational Drawings			•		•		•		•
I-6 Hide and Seek	•	•	•		•	•	•		•
I-7 Zoo Murals		•		•	•				•
I-8 Scratchboards	•		•		•		•		•
I-9 Imagination Machines	•	•				•	•		•
Section II: Painting									
II-1 Giant Paper Ice Cream Cones	•	•		•			•		•
II-2 Pussy Willows	•	•	•	•	•	•			•
II-3 Sidewalk Paintings	•	•		•				•	•
II-4 Painted Skeletons	•	•				•		•	•
II-5 Big Bad Bug Painting	•	•		•	•	•	•		•
II-6 Painted Turkeys	•	•		•	•	•	•		•
II-7 Glowing Fish	•	•	•	•	•	•	•		•
II-8 Fabric Painting	•	•	•	•			•	•	•
Section III: Color and Design									
III-1 Letter Pictures	•	•					•		•
III-2 Horizontal and Vertical Designs	•		•	•			•		•
III-3 Crayon Picture Puzzles	•	•	•	•		•	•		•
III-4 Photograms	•	•	•				•		•
III-5 All-Over Patterns	•	•	•				•		•
III-6 One Shape Only	•	•	•				•		•
III-7 Crayon Fireworks	•	•	•		•		•		•
III-8 Pattern Birds	•	•			•	•	•		•
III-9 Line Art	•		•				•		•
III-10 Word Pictures	•	•	•	•			•		•
III-11 Sunglasses		•		•			•		•
III-12 Collage Portraits	•	•		•	•	•	•	•	•
III-13 Costume Collage		•			•	•	•		•
Section IV: Ceramics									
IV-1 Clay Candlesticks	•	•			•		•	•	•
IV-2 Ceramic Coil Mirrors	•	•			•				•
IV-3 Clay Face Necklaces		•			•	•			•
IV-4 Heart Frames and Necklaces	•	•		•	•		•		•
IV-5 Clay Bells		•		•	•		•		•
IV-6 Clay Pockets		•			•		•		•
IV-7 Coil Pottery	•	•			•		•	•	•
IV-8 Clay Appliqué Plaques	•	•		•	•		•		•
IV-9 Evergreen Plaques	•	•	•		•		•		•

Focus Areas

	line	shape	value	color	texture	perspective & proportion	pattern & composition	cultural enrichment	creative thinking
Section V: Paper Crafts									
V-1 Torn Paper Trees	●	●		●	●	●	●		●
V-2 Paper Bag Houses		●		●		●			●
V-3 Stitched Paper Puppets	●	●		●		●		●	●
V-4 Quilling Valentines	●	●			●	●	●	●	●
V-5 Paper Sculpture Animals		●		●	●	●			●
V-6 Witches	●	●		●	●	●			●
V-7 Oaktag Houses	●	●				●		●	●
V-8 Tissue Paper Fish Kites		●				●	●	●	●
V-9 Two-Cardboard Relief	●	●	●	●	●		●		●
V-10 Dancing Bears	●	●				●			●
V-11 Landscape in the Round	●	●		●	●	●			●
V-12 Lunar Shadow Boxes	●	●	●	●	●	●			●
V-13 Paper Bag People		●		●	●	●			●
V-14 Tissue Paper Silhouettes	●	●	●			●		●	●
Section VI: Printmaking									
VI-1 Handprints	●	●			●				●
VI-2 Texture Prints	●	●	●	●	●		●	●	●
VI-3 Chalk Prints		●	●	●			●		●
VI-4 Two-Color Styrofoam Prints	●	●	●	●	●		●		●
VI-5 Tempera Tile Prints	●	●	●	●	●		●		●
VI-6 Leaf Prints	●	●	●		●		●		●
VI-7 Gadget Prints	●	●	●	●	●		●		●
Section VII: Weaving									
VII-1 Straight Weaving	●			●	●		●	●	●
VII-2 Circle Weaving	●	●	●	●	●		●	●	●
VII-3 Paper Weaving	●	●	●	●	●		●	●	●
VII-4 Ojos de Dios	●		●	●	●		●	●	●
VII-5 Straw Weaving	●	●	●	●	●		●	●	●
Section VIII: Crafts									
VIII-1 Stuffed Butterflies		●		●		●	●		●
VIII-2 Planetary Architecture	●	●		●	●	●			●
VIII-3 Point-to-Point Yarn Designs	●	●		●			●		●
VIII-4 Soft Foam Masks	●	●		●	●	●		●	●
VIII-5 Constructional Problem Solving	●	●	●				●		●
VIII-6 Complete the Picture		●	●			●			●
VIII-7 Wood Sculpture	●	●		●	●	●	●		●
VIII-8 Hand Puppets		●		●	●	●		●	●
VIII-9 Aluminum Plaster Casting	●		●		●			●	●
VIII-10 Metal Masks	●	●		●		●			●

Focus Areas

	line	shape	value	color	texture	perspective & proportion	pattern & composition	cultural enrichment	creative thinking
Section I: Drawing									
I-1 Action Figures	●	●				●			●
I-2 Pen and Ink Owls	●	●	●		●	●	●	●	●
I-3 Two-Pencil Drawings	●	●	●				●		●
I-4 Musical Still Life	●	●		●		●	●	●	●
I-5 Personality Profiles	●	●	●			●	●	●	●
I-6 Window Views	●	●	●	●		●	●	●	●
I-7 Half-Face Portraits	●	●	●		●	●		●	●
I-8 Whale Dreams	●	●				●			●
I-9 Architecture in Our Town	●	●			●	●		●	●
I-10 Portraiture	●	●	●	●	●	●		●	●
I-11 Two-Point Perspective	●	●				●		●	●
I-12 Bicycle Drawings	●	●				●	●		●
I-13 Texture Drawings	●	●	●		●		●		●
I-14 Idiomatic Illustrations	●	●		●					●
Section II: Painting									
II-1 Foil Clowns	●	●		●	●				●
II-2 Window Portraits	●	●		●	●	●			●
II-3 Jungle Resist	●	●	●	●	●	●	●		●
II-4 Pointillism		●	●	●			●	●	●
II-5 Sand Paintings		●		●	●			●	●
II-6 Warm and Cool Colors		●	●	●		●		●	●
II-7 Monochromatic Painting		●	●	●		●		●	●
II-8 Multimedia Slides	●	●	●	●	●		●		●
Section III: Color and Design									
III-1 Art Object Designs	●	●	●	●			●		●
III-2 Magazine Textures	●	●	●		●	●	●		●
III-3 Paper Mosaic		●	●	●	●		●	●	●
III-4 Geometric Pictures	●	●	●	●			●		●
III-5 Rainbow Pictures	●	●		●			●		●
III-6 Multimedia Mosaic	●	●	●	●	●		●		●
III-7 Negative/Positive Designs	●	●	●				●		●
III-8 Design a Van	●	●		●		●			●
III-9 Candy Jars	●	●		●		●		●	●
III-10 One Line Only	●	●	●		●		●		●
III-11 Color and Design	●	●	●	●			●		●
III-12 Radial Designs	●	●	●	●			●		●
III-13 Optical Illusions	●	●	●				●		●
III-14 Lettering	●	●					●		●

Focus Areas

	line	shape	value	color	texture	perspective & proportion	pattern & composition	cultural enrichment	creative thinking
Section IV: Ceramics									
IV-1 Clay Mobiles		•		•	•		•		•
IV-2 Treasure Boxes	•	•		•	•		•		•
IV-3 Clay Dinosaurs		•		•	•	•		•	•
IV-4 Clay Houses	•	•		•	•	•			•
IV-5 Clay Animals	•	•		•	•	•			•
IV-6 Dream Car	•	•		•	•	•	•		•
IV-7 Clay People	•	•		•	•	•			•
Section V: Paper Crafts									
V-1 Setting the Stage for Halloween	•	•		•	•	•			•
V-2 Halloween Mobiles	•	•		•			•	•	•
V-3 Three-Dimensional Silhouettes	•	•	•			•			•
V-4 Cut Paper Masterpiece	•	•	•	•		•	•	•	•
V-5 Paper Towers	•	•	•	•			•		•
V-6 Kites	•	•		•			•		•
V-7 Colonial Pull Toys	•	•		•		•	•	•	•
V-8 Flying Tetrahedrons	•	•					•		•
Section VI: Printmaking									
VI-1 Styrofoam Texture Prints	•	•	•	•	•		•	•	•
VI-2 Linoleum Block Prints	•	•	•	•	•		•	•	•
VI-3 Silk-Screen Prints	•	•	•	•			•		•
VI-4 Glue Prints	•	•	•	•			•		•
Section VII: Weaving									
VII-1 Op-Art Weaving	•	•	•				•		•
VII-2 People Weavings	•		•	•	•		•	•	•
VII-3 Textural Weaving	•	•	•	•	•		•	•	•
VII-4 Basket Weaving	•	•			•		•	•	•
Section VIII: Crafts									
VIII-1 Puppet on a String		•		•	•	•		•	•
VIII-2 Papier-mâché Flu Bugs		•		•	•	•		•	•
VIII-3 Fluorocarbon Foam Sculpture	•		•		•			•	•
VIII-4 Creative Problem Solving	•	•	•	•	•		•		•
VIII-5 Gnomes	•			•	•	•			•
VIII-6 Milk Jug Masks	•	•		•	•	•			•
VIII-7 Butterfly Batik	•	•	•	•			•	•	•
VIII-8 Copper Foil Jewelry	•	•					•	•	•
VIII-9 Robots	•	•		•	•	•			•
VIII-10 Balsa Wood Houses	•	•		•					•
VIII-11 Marionettes	•			•	•	•		•	•
VIII-12 Sand Casting	•	•			•		•	•	•
VIII-13 Clone Soft Sculpture		•		•	•	•			•
VIII-14 Creativity Kits	•	•	•		•		•	•	•
VIII-15 Animation	•	•	•	•				•	•
VIII-16 Zodiac Banners	•	•	•	•	•	•	•		•

ART CURRICULUM ACTIVITIES KITS
Primary Level

Level 1

The first activity in this chapter introduces and explores the *Self-Portrait* and demonstrates the important role observation skills play in creating realistic drawings. *Body Portraits* is a large-as-life lesson that concentrates on the use of contour lines in figure drawings. The narrative nature of drawing is examined in *Castle Drawings*, a lesson which also introduces the technique of cross-sectioning.

Self-Portrait

Level 2

The Royal Portrait is a simplified introduction to formal compositional elements. In *Motivational Drawings*, creative drawing from imagination is emphasized. *Hide and Seek* is a lesson that imaginatively demonstrates how overlapping can be used in a drawing to create the illusion of depth. It is also a lesson in developing an eye for detail. The *Zoo Mural* introduces the mural as an art form and shows how found objects and other materials can be combined to create a collage.

Hide and Seek

Level 3

In *Scratchboards*, different types of lines and their various characteristics are examined. *Imagination Machines* is a lesson that encourages the students to apply the same eye for detail employed in drawings from life to their drawings from imagination.

Scratchboards

Self-Portrait

SELF-PORTRAIT

Materials:

- 12″ × 18″ white paper
- scissors
- 12″ × 18″ black paper
- crayons

Directions:

1. Think of the three main parts of your body: your head, your trunk, and your legs.
2. Your head is connected to your trunk by your neck, which is almost as wide as your head.
3. Shoulders are on top of your trunk and are about twice as wide as your head.
4. At the ends of the shoulders the arms begin, and they can bend in half at the elbow.
5. Don't forget hands and fingers.
6. The legs begin from the bottom of the trunk and can bend in half at the knee.
7. Don't forget about feet and toes.
8. Think about your own special features: What color hair and eyes do you have? Is your hair long or short, curly or straight? Do you have bangs, or do you wear your hair tied in some way or with barrettes? Do you wear glasses?
9. What kind and color of clothes do you have on today? What about your shoes?
10. Begin to draw yourself as large as possible vertically on the white paper and remember all the items you have thought about.
11. When you have finished, cut out your picture and glue it onto the black paper. Remember to squeeze the glue on the back of the white paper in a little line of glue running near the edge of the paper.

Body Portraits

BODY PORTRAITS

Materials:

- thin, black marker
- 36″ × 4′ piece of paper
- tempera paint and brushes
- scissors

Directions:

1. Lay paper on floor or table.
2. Lay down on the paper and assume any position you want. Try to have your arms and legs separated, but do not lay them across your body.
3. Have someone trace slowly and completely around you with a marker showing your complete outline.

4. Get up and complete the "inside" of the drawing, adding lines for clothes and shoes, a face, and a line where the hair surrounds the face.
5. Paint in with tempera.
6. When dry, cut out.

Castle Drawings

CASTLE DRAWINGS

Materials:

- 12″ × 18″ white drawing paper
- pencil and eraser
- thin, black marker

Directions:

1. Think of what the back of a doll house looks like—all open so that you can see into all the rooms at the same time. This is called a cross-section.
2. Think of what a castle looks like—walls, towers, battlements, gateways, an interior with stairs.
3. Draw a castle this same way showing all the rooms: a banquet hall and kitchen, a dungeon, the throne room, some bedrooms, an entrance hall, and any other type of room you may think would have been found in a castle.
4. Add people doing various jobs in all the rooms to make the castle life run smoothly.
5. Add furniture, rugs, or banners hanging on the walls, and swords and shields for decorations.

Royal Portrait

ROYAL PORTRAIT

Materials:

- 1 sheet of construction paper, 12″ × 18″
- pencil and eraser
- thin, black marker
- crayons
- various examples of royal portraits (for example, *The Old King*, by Georges Rouault, a king and queen from a deck of cards)

Directions:

1. What do you notice about the way kings and queens are portrayed? Do these portraits seem serious or silly? Do the people seem stiff or relaxed? How do you know whether the person in the picture is a king or queen?

2. Answering the questions in step 1 will help you with your own Royal Portraits. Begin by creating the face for your king or queen with pencil on construction paper. Add the features of the face carefully. Try to make an expression that is similar to the ones you have observed.

3. After completing the face, you may add the hair and crown. Try to show as much detail as possible. For example, perhaps you could add the king/queen's jewels in your crown or a beard and mustache for the king.

4. To complete your portrait, you may wish to show his or her collar. Is it velvet? fur? satin?

5. When you are happy with your drawing, go over your pencil lines with a thin, black marker. Then begin to color your king or queen with crayons. Remember some colors can look more "royal" than others. Which ones? Why?

Motivational Drawings

MOTIVATIONAL DRAWINGS

Materials:

- 12″ × 18″ white drawing paper
- thin, black marker

Directions:

1. Far away in outer space there exists the planet ROM. On this magnificent planet live the Roms and their cousins the Nats, who are evil and look very different from the Roms.

2. Now I have never seen a Rom, nor have I been to ROM, but I've heard that both of these creatures are something to behold.

3. They move and communicate by the most amazing means, and they can change their forms whenever they wish.

4. Most of them are large; some are tall.

5. You have been assigned to travel to this planet and draw pictures of the creatures, because they are allergic to cameras and get very sick if one is pointed at them.

6. Draw your idea of a Rom and your idea of a Nat.

Hide and Seek

HIDE AND SEEK

Materials:

- white drawing paper
- pencils and erasers
- thin, black markers
- crayons

Directions:

1. Have you ever played Hide and Go Seek? Well, pretend you're "it." You are counting to 100; you have your hands over your eyes, and you are lying in a field of tall grass. Now, when you get to 50, you might start to peek through your fingers a little, and as you do, you notice the world of "tiny" things right under your nose. In this "tiny" world, the grass seems very tall compared to the size of an ant or a ladybug. Why, to an ant, one blade of grass might seem like Mt. Everest! In your pictures, try to capture as many different "creatures" as possible. Just make sure that none of them are too large. Some of the things you might include are pebbles, mushrooms, spider webs, flowers, clover, snails, butterflies, worms, spiders, caterpillars, grasshoppers, baby turtles, frogs, ladybugs, ants, beetles, centipedes, flies, and bumblebees. It's quite a busy world, even though it's a tiny one.

2. Holding your paper horizontally, begin to draw your grass. Make lines from the bottom to the top to show individual blades of grass. Some will be straight, some will be bent, some will be short, some will be long, some will be fat, some will be skinny. Most will be skinnier on the top than at the bottom. And in order to show a lot of grass in your picture, some blades of grass will have to go behind others. When this happens, simply stop your line where it meets another blade of grass and start it again on the other side. This step takes some practice, so keep your eraser handy.

3. After you have drawn as many layers as possible, outline them carefully with a thin, black marker and make sure you stay on your pencil outlines.

4. Next, use your pencil to add insects and other tiny things. Then, outline these with a marker, too.

5. Afterward, you can begin coloring in, and you may want to make your grass different shades of green. This can look very interesting when completed.

6. Your teacher may wish to display several of your pictures together when they're done. Together they can create a giant grass jungle!

Zoo Murals

ZOO MURALS

Materials:

- long piece of mural strength paper
- scrap papers of all kinds, including wallpaper, glazed paper, fluorescent paper, velour paper, metallic paper, magazines
- scissors and glue
- thin, colored markers
- 12″ × 18″ manila paper
- pencil and eraser

(Note: This is suggested as a group project.)

Directions:

1. Draw an animal that lives at the zoo.
2. Add a protective environment to keep him away from people and people away from him, but do not use a fence or a cage. Rocks, water, and gulleys can serve this purpose.
3. Adjust the environment to your animal's needs. Does he like to climb, to swim, to run? Are there places for him to hide and have privacy when he wants it?
4. Cut your animal out of the appropriate color paper.
5. Do the same for his environment.
6. Glue the animal on his environment.
7. Glue the animal and his environment on the long pieces of mural paper.
8. Add other animals and their environments.
9. Add other items for further interest such as the following: people walking, viewing the animals, and taking pictures; sidewalks; signs; trees; bushes; ticket booths; refreshment stands; and so forth.

Scratchboards

SCRATCHBOARDS

Materials:

- 9″ × 12″ sheet of oaktag or poster board
- regular and fluorescent crayons
- black tempera and brushes
- liquid dish detergent
- sharp, wooden stick
- newspaper
- manila paper

Directions:

1. Begin by drawing random shapes on the oaktag and coloring them in by pressing very hard on the crayons.

2. When this is completed, prepare your paint by adding a few drops of liquid detergent and stirring carefully. Then place your paper on top of the newspaper and brush the black paint across it in slow, even strokes. Continue this until your paper is completely black. Then put it aside to dry.

3. While it is drying, you may wish to make a practice sketch and experiment with some of the effects you can create with different types of lines in your scratchboard. See the following examples.

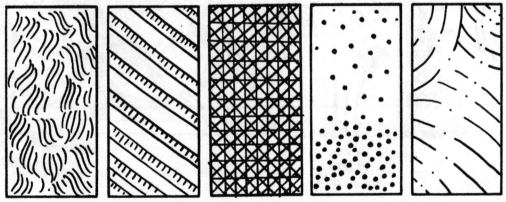

4. Once the paint has dried, you can start to "scratch" your picture into the black surface with a sharp, wooden stick. The unexpected colors will surprise you as they are revealed in your picture.

Imagination Machines

IMAGINATION MACHINES

Materials:

- 12″ × 18″ white paper
- pencil and eraser
- thin, black marker
- cardboard cogs, wheels, circles, rectangles, and cylindrically shaped patterns

Directions:

1. Think of all the machines that do jobs for us (vacuum cleaners, refrigerators, sewing machines) and that make life easier. What jobs or tasks do you do now that you would like a machine to do?
2. Look at machines in your school, that is, typewriters, movie projectors, and so forth.
3. Observe a collection of "machine-making stuff" including cardboard cogs and wheels in various sizes, circles, tabs, various rectangular shapes, and pipes.
4. Use black markers to draw around these shapes.

5. Add these parts together and continue with your own.
6. A "making" machine needs a place to put something in and a place for the finished product to come out, with lots of "stuff" in the middle to do the making.
7. A "doing" machine might need special switches and arms to control it and make it do its work.
8. Label your paper with the task your machine performs.

Level 1

Sidewalk Paintings

Painting on a large scale, combining simple shapes, and creating a pattern through repetition are all involved in *Giant Paper Ice Cream Cones.* The next activity, *Pussy Willows,* combines drawing and painting. Students learn more about creating depth in their work when faced with the task of showing overlapping branches as they appear through a transparent surface. *Sidewalk Paintings* is an activity that encourages large, bold expression using bright colors and simple shapes.

Level 2

Big Bad Bug Painting

Most paintings begin with a drawing, but in the lesson *Painted Skeletons,* students learn to build up their paintings using directly painted shapes. Fantasy and imagination are stressed in the next activity, *Big Bad Bug Paintings.* Outlining with black paint, using primary colors, and reducing complex objects to simple forms are all involved in *Painted Turkeys.*

Level 3

Glowing Fish

Pattern, repetition, and texture are explored using fluorescent paint on black paper to create *Glowing Fish.* In *Fabric Painting,* students are encouraged to become their own designer and create some wearable art.

Giant Paper Ice Cream Cones

GIANT PAPER ICE CREAM CONES

Materials:

- pencil and eraser
- 12" × 18" paper
- crayons
- glue
- scissors

Directions:

1. Think of your favorite flavor of ice cream and the fun of eating ice cream on a hot summer day.
2. Begin by drawing a triangle on the paper for the cone.
3. Cut this out.
4. Draw curved, straight, or zigzag lines across the cone and then down like a real ice cream cone design.
5. The shapes resulting from the crossed lines can be colored in brightly.
6. Think of the shape of a scoop of ice cream. Is it a plain, round ball? Imagine a big, fluffy scoop, the kind that hangs over the side of the cone. Make some curves, some bumps, some wiggles.

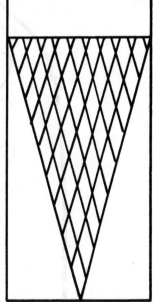

7. Cut these out. If you have trouble, cut down into the points of your ice cream scoops by first cutting down one side, then removing the scissors and cutting down the other side, rather than trying to cut down and then up.
8. Draw and cut out another smaller scoop.
9. Glue all three parts together and add a cherry on top.
10. Add treats to your scoops: cherries and berries, nuts and chocolate bits, marshmallow fluffs, strings of licorice, hearts, sprinkles.

Pussy Willows

PUSSY WILLOWS

Materials:

- 12″ × 18″ gray paper
- thin, black marker
- glass vase of pussy willows
- silver crayons
- cotton swabs
- white tempera paint

Directions:

1. After viewing the vase of pussy willows for a few minutes, place your paper vertically in front of you.
2. Draw in the vase with your marker.
3. Next, add all of the branches using a silver crayon.
4. Make sure your willows stretch nearly to the top of your paper.
5. Dab on the pussy willow buds with a cotton swab dipped in white tempera.

Sidewalk Paintings

SIDEWALK PAINTINGS

Materials:

- sidewalk or playground-surfaced area
- powdered tempera paints or large mural chalk
- plastic buckets to mix and carry paint
- large brushes
- white chalk

Directions:

1. Using the white chalk, draw the outlines of objects you wish to paint. Make them large and simple for this larger-than-life painting.
2. Mix four or five basic colors in the buckets to a cream soup consistency.
3. The best colors to use are white, red, orange, yellow, and green. Avoid blues, purples, and black because these colors are long lasting.
4. Begin to paint in the objects.
5. Have one bucket of clean water handy to clean brushes.
6. Do not paint over and over the same spot (built-up paint may come off on shoes).
7. If using chalk, let it soak first in water and then color in the objects as before.
8. Let dry and enjoy.
9. When you are tired of your painting, use a hose and a stiff bristle brush broom to remove. Brush stubborn spots with a little liquid soap. Paint will not harm grass.

Painted Skeletons

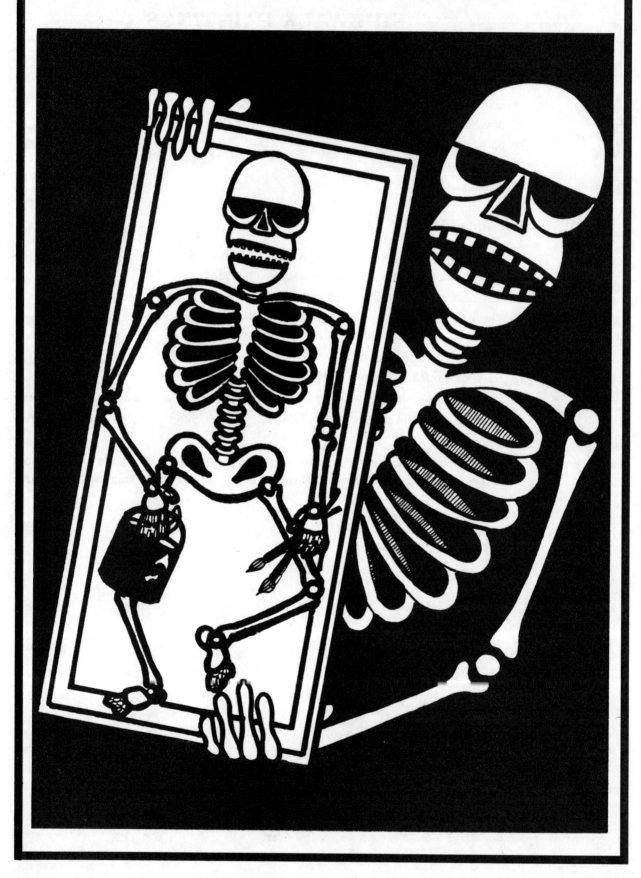

PAINTED SKELETONS

Materials:

- black construction paper
- white tempera paint
- thin paintbrush

Directions:

1. These skeletons are quite simple to make when you think of them as a collection of simple shapes.

2. Begin at the top of your paper by outlining a half circle and then fill it in with paint. Outline a triangle but do not fill this in.

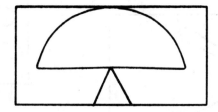

3. Next, outline two loops from the base of the triangle to each side of the half circle.

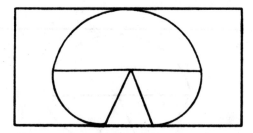

4. Then add another half circle to the base of the triangle and fill it in. Make another one (upside down) a few inches below that and also fill it in.

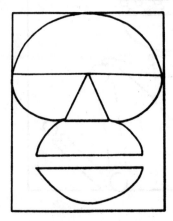 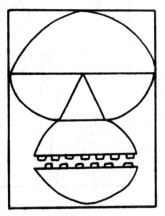

5. Next, use your brush to make small lines coming out of each half circle; these are the teeth.

6. To make your neck, add a rectangle to the bottom of your half circle with small lines sticking out of the sides.

7. Next, make the collar bone by painting a "flattened" V. Add a small circle at each end of the V. We use circles to show that two bones meet and that they can move in different directions because of "joints." Imagine how your arms would work if there were no joints! Can you feel the joint by your shoulder? Where are some other joints?

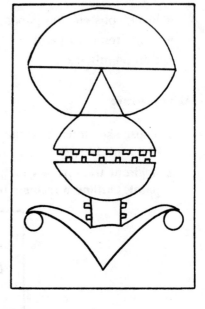

8. Paint a line to show the upper arm and then an elbow joint, then your lower arm and your wrist joint.

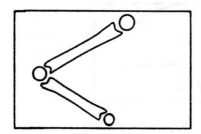

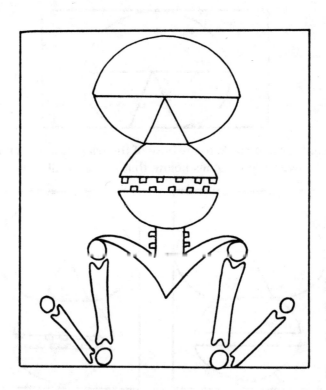

9. You can make a hand by painting a half circle and adding thin lines to show each finger. How many joints will each finger have? If you can't show all three joints, just make as many as you can.

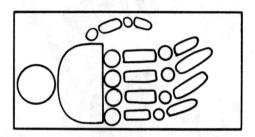

10. To create the chest, extend a line down from the center of your collar bone and show your ribs with a series of loops. Notice how the loops get smaller and smaller. Can you find your ribs? How many do you have? Try to show that many if you can.

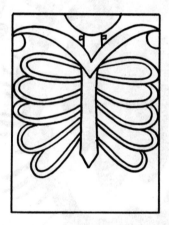

11. Next, extend your body by including a line for your spine and a flattened pear shape to show your hip bone.

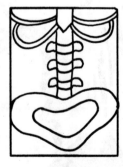

12. You can add your legs in the same way you added your arms. Remember your legs can "bend" wherever there is a "joint." Your skeleton can be shown running or jumping or just standing still.

13. Add your feet by showing the heel and the sole and the toes with all their joints.

Big Bad Bug Painting

BIG BAD BUG PAINTING

Materials:

- tempera and brushes
- 12″ × 18″ white drawing paper

Directions:

1. Think about what "bad" means to you.
2. What do you see when you hear the word "bug"—a germ or an insect?
3. How can you show that something is "big" in a painting?
4. What could a bad bug be doing? Biting someone to give the flu, sliding down someone's throat to give him or her a sore throat, fighting inside someone's body?
5. Your bug does not have to look anything like a real bug, but it might.
6. If it is an insect, it could be fighting other bugs, tearing a nest down, or biting its prey.

Painted Turkeys

PAINTED TURKEYS

Materials:

- pencil and eraser
- tempera paint and brush
- 36″ × 40″ heavy yellow paper
- 9″ × 12″ paper

Directions:

1. Draw a large circle on the 9″ × 12″ paper and a smaller circle next to it connected by two lines as shown.

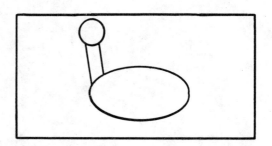

2. Add a beak, one eye, wings, a waddle, legs, and feet as shown (remember that a bird's knees bend backwards!).

3. Add overlapping ovals for feathers as shown. Three rows are usually enough.

4. Using your 9″ × 12″ drawing as a guide, draw the turkey again on a piece of yellow 36″ × 40″ paper and make your drawing large enough so that part of the turkey touches each edge of the paper. Notice how simple geometric shapes can be combined to create an object.

5. Go over all pencil lines with a brush and black tempera.

6. When dry, paint in the sections and the body with other colors, or let some sections remain the yellow color of the paper.

Glowing Fish

GLOWING FISH

Materials:

- 12″ × 18″ manila paper
- 12″ × 18″ black paper
- fluorescent paint and brushes
- pencil and eraser

Directions:

1. Draw a basic fish shape on the manila paper. Use your own idea or one as shown.

2. Include designs to add interest to the fish, such as scallops, zigzags, stars, polka dots, and so forth.

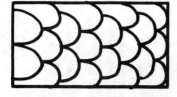 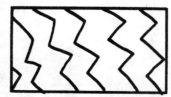 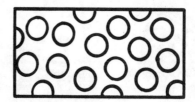

3. You might also add fancy fins or flowing tail pieces.
4. Transfer your drawing to the black paper.
5. Begin painting in the designs and the outline of the fish. Leave the inside of the body black.

Fabric Painting

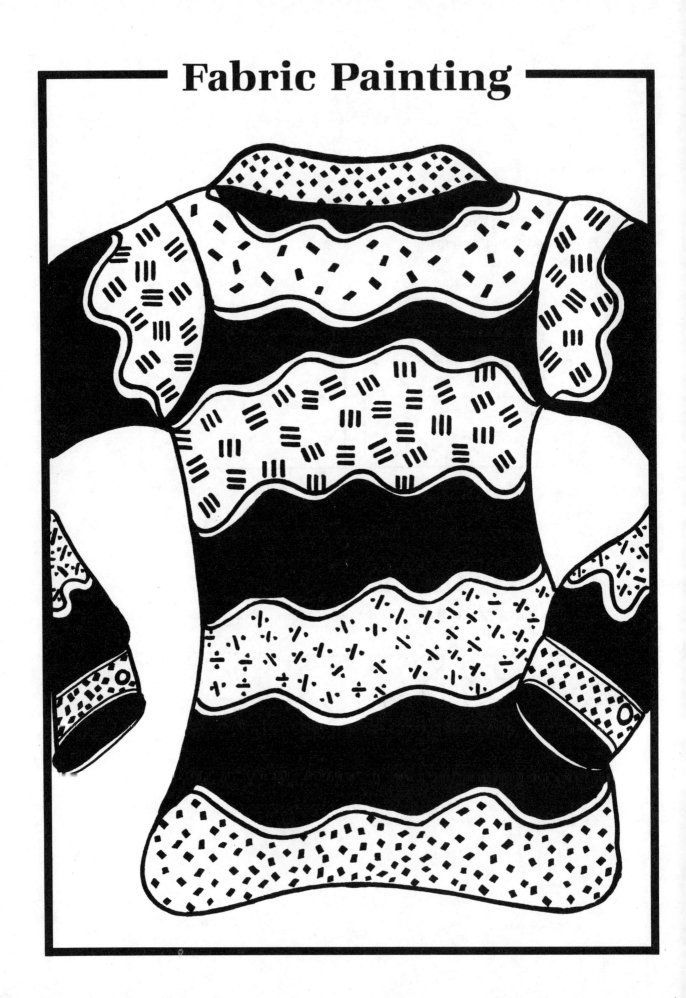

FABRIC PAINTING

Materials:

- polyester shirt
- fabric paint or markers
- 9″ × 12″ paper
- black marker
- brushes

Directions:

1. Clothing has been designed and patterned in different ways for interest and decoration by people all over the world and throughout the ages.

2. Remember that a pattern is a design, line, or shape that is repeated.

3. Fold your paper in half, then in half again and again until you have eight rectangles.

4. In each rectangle, front and back, draw a different pattern so that you end up with sixteen patterns.

5. You can have lines that zigzag or scallop and shapes of different sizes, or combinations of these.

6. Notice how your shirt is made up of a variety of pieces: the cuffs, the sleeves, the yoke, the collar, two front pieces, and the back. You probably have at least nine different pieces which have been sewn together to make your shirt.

7. Using the fabric paint or markers, copy one pattern from your paper onto one piece or section of your shirt.

8. Repeat the pattern carefully for the full length of the shirt.

9. Try changing the colors of paint or markers for variety.

10. Continue until all the shirt pieces are completed with different patterns from your practice paper.

11. Let dry and wear proudly.

Color and Design

Level 1

Letter Pictures is an activity that asks students to consider the letter as an element of design and to combine these new designs to create a picture. *Horizontal and Vertical Designs* is an activity that demonstrates the design possibilities in even the simplest combination of lines. Reinforcing the concept of how parts make a whole is given prominence in *Crayon Picture Puzzles.* Nature as an art form is considered in *Photograms,* which also encourages students to organize the elements of their composition. *All Over Patterns* deals with repetition as the necessary ingredient in creating patterns.

Photograms

Level 2

One Shape Only clearly defines the use of geometric shapes in creating pictures. In this lesson, students learn about diversity (using one shape to compose each element in their picture) and also about repetition (repeating the same shape to create a new shape). Overlapping to create the illusion of depth, repetition of line patterns to create an explosive effect, and learning to contrast colors to give a design more impact are all involved in the lesson *Crayon Fireworks.*

Crayon Fireworks

Level 3

In the lesson *Pattern Birds,* students are encouraged to explore different ways to represent texture through the use of design. In *Line Art,* the character and quality of different types of lines are examined.

Word Pictures are just what they sound like, pictures composed entirely of words. *Sunglasses* is a lesson which incorporates fantasy with simple product design. By reducing a face to simple shapes and using a variety of different materials to create those shapes, students will be creating *Collage Portraits.* In *Costume Collage* students design their work by carefully selecting and combining different types of materials and patterns.

Costume Collage

Letter Pictures

LETTER PICTURES

Materials:

- magazines (especially weekly news magazines with big advertising letters)
- scissors
- glue
- 9″ × 12″ paper
- crayons

Directions:

1. Cut out various large letters from magazine ads.
2. Lay a few at a time on your paper and imagine how each could be part of an animal or a person: maybe a body, ears, a trunk, or a tail.
3. Lay the letters on their sides, or upside down, or backward until they remind you of part of something.
4. The letters that most resemble a face are "C," "D," "O," and "U."
5. It is a good idea to use the largest letters for the body and smaller letters for details.
6. The letters are not important as long as they are arranged in the shape of a body.
7. Use your crayons to add details and to fill in the background.
8. Details are important; they help to identify the subject.
9. Remember that there should be a foreground and background to your picture.
10. Too many small objects on the paper distract from the center of interest. Develop one large image and add to it with your crayons.
11. Do not glue until finished.

Horizontal and Vertical Designs

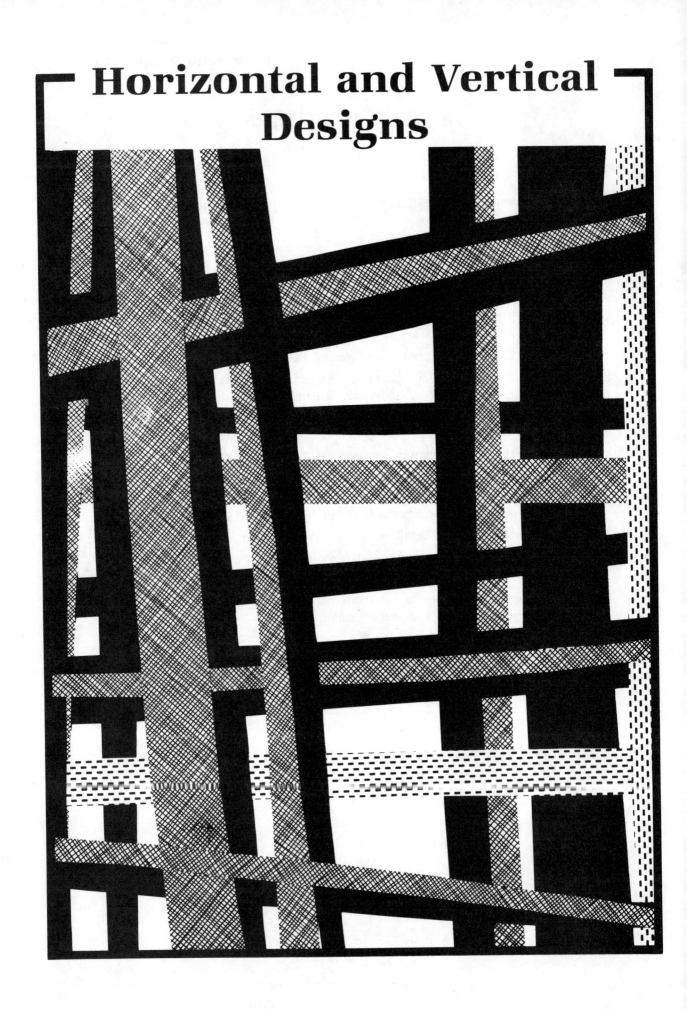

HORIZONTAL AND VERTICAL DESIGNS

Materials:

- 1 sheet of white or black construction paper, 12" × 18"
- thin strips of construction paper in various colors
- paste or white glue
- scissors

Directions:

1. Horizontal lines are ones that go across and vertical lines go up and down. Look around your classroom and see how many you can find. Can a person be a horizontal or vertical line? When?

2. Cut strips of construction paper in all different colors. Make some of your strips wide and some thin, some long and some short.

3. Now begin to place these strips on top of either a white or black sheet of construction paper. Arrange all the strips so that they are either horizontal or vertical lines.

4. Experiment with your strips and try to create interesting shapes with them. When you are happy with your arrangement, carefully paste or glue all your strips in place.

Crayon Picture Puzzles

CRAYON PICTURE PUZZLES

Materials:

- 9" × 12" sheet of thin shirt cardboard
- colored markers or crayons
- pencil and eraser
- sharp scissors

Directions:

1. Discuss what makes some ideas for pictures best for puzzles: some big shapes, definite lines (easier to match), variety in sizes of shapes and in colors.
2. Draw a picture on the cardboard and color it in using the markers.
3. Cut your picture up into irregular puzzle pieces.
4. Include some difficult pieces such as the ones shown.

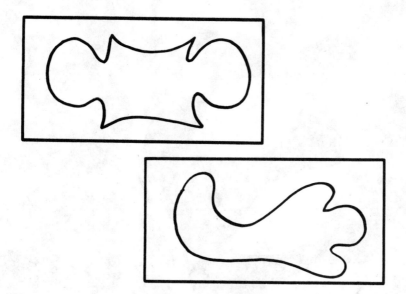

5. Some rounded bumps and uneven places help make the puzzle more fun. Sharp, thin points should be avoided because they are easily broken.

Photograms

PHOTOGRAMS

Materials:

- blueprint paper
- small, fairly flat objects from nature: grasses, leaves, flowers, weeds, feathers, and so forth
- shallow pan of water
- 12″ × 18″ blue construction paper folded in half like a book
- a magazine

Directions:

1. For practice, arrange the objects into a design on the cover of the folded construction paper "book." Lay objects on the blueprint paper in a fairly dark room and close the magazine.
2. Carry the magazine, keeping it flat, outside on a sunny day.
3. Carefully open the magazine, on the ground, to your blueprint paper and the sun will begin to change the color of the paper, while the paper under the objects will remain light.
4. You may want to try moving the objects slightly to one side or another as the fading takes place for a transparent effect.
5. Depending on the kind of blueprint paper you use, you can prevent your designs from fading away. Some paper may simply be wet with water and others may be fixed in a "photographic stop fix bath."

All-Over Patterns

ALL-OVER PATTERNS

Materials:

- tempera/brushes
- 18″ × 24″ construction paper

Directions:

1. Think of what it means to repeat something: to make the same thing over and over.
2. Think of what a pattern is: a repetition of a shape, a line, a design, or a color.
3. Think of how repetition and pattern occur in nature: bark, flowers, rainbows, fish, birds, insects, snowflakes, the insides of fruits and vegetables.
4. Think of how they are used by people: in fabric, wallpaper, clothes, rugs, jewelry.
5. Fold your piece of construction paper in half, then in half again. Continue first in one direction, then in another to form a grid or network of polygonal units.
6. Enter a single line or shape in one unit and repeat it in all the others.
7. Paint a new design element in the first unit: Another line? Another shape? An area colored in?
8. Repeat this element again in all the others.
9. Continue building up the design in this way—with lines, shapes, colors, accents, details—until you have an all-over pattern.
10. Mount or frame the finished pattern with another colored piece of construction paper.

One Shape Only

ONE SHAPE ONLY

Materials:

- 12″ × 18″ colored construction paper
- glue
- scissors
- pencil and eraser
- construction paper scraps

Directions:

1. Pick one basic geometric shape: circle, rectangle, triangle, or diamond.

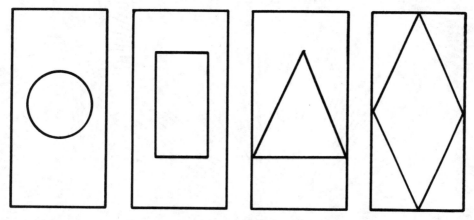

2. Cut various sizes and types of your shape in order to assemble objects to make a picture.

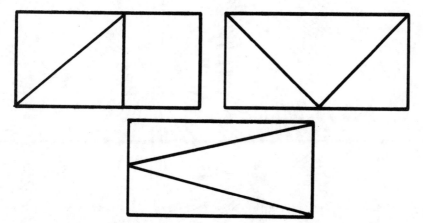

3. Once a shape has been chosen, all objects in the picture must be made from that shape; no other shape can be introduced.

Crayon Fireworks

CRAYON FIREWORKS

Materials:

- crayons
- manila paper

Directions:

1. Begin by making a dot anywhere on your paper.

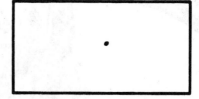

2. From your dot, draw four short lines. Put one line at the top, one at the bottom, and one line on each side. All your lines should be the same color and the same length.

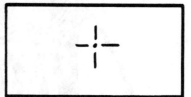

3. Now add four more lines, one inside each space created by your first four lines.

4. If there is any space left between these lines, add a few more.

5. You have just completed one "explosion" of your crayon fireworks. To make it stand out, keep adding more exploding rings around the first one, but use a new color each time you start a new ring.

6. Build up each ring the same way you did for your first one.

7. When you have completed one of the fireworks, then you can add another by placing a dot somewhere else on your paper. As your paper fills up, you'll notice that some of the fireworks will have to overlap. This overlapping makes your fireworks look very exciting, as if one were bursting right after the other.

Pattern Birds

PATTERN BIRDS

Materials:

- 9″ × 12″ paper
- 12″ × 18″ black paper
- thin, black markers
- oil pastels
- pencil and eraser

Directions:

1. What is a pattern? Look at the designs in the clothes you are wearing. The shapes are repeated—this is a pattern. Patterns add interest to objects in our lives—clothing, draperies, furniture, and so forth.

2. Fold a 9″ × 12″ piece of paper into eight rectangles.

3. Using a thin, black marker, draw a different repeated shape or design in each to make a different pattern in each.

4. Using a pencil, draw an imaginary bird vertically on a 12″ × 18″ black piece of paper. As long as it has a beak, a tail, wings, and "bird" feet, it will look like a bird. What different shapes can a beak be? What about the body of a bird?

5. Birds' legs are different from ours. Our knees bend forward—birds' knees bend backward. They also have four toes—three come forward and one short one is backward to help the birds balance.

5. Divide the bird into eight sections.

6. Draw a different pattern in each section.

7. Trace over the patterns and the outline of the bird with oil pastels.

8. You may want to color in certain areas completely.

Line Art

LINE ART

Materials:

- markers
- oil crayons
- 9″ × 12″ brightly colored paper

Directions:

1. Look for lines in your environment—branches, railroad tracks, roads, telephone wires, veins in a leaf, lines in a person's face, and so forth.

2. There are many kinds of lines: straight, curved, jagged, coiled, broken, heavy, delicate, and so forth.

3. Lines in a painting or a drawing serve a variety of purposes: to define shapes, to link two points, to create a path of motion in a painting, to decorate, and to create a mood.

4. In an artwork, a line can be represented by materials such as wire in a sculpture or yarn in a weaving.

5. Draw on a piece of scratch paper the following lines: a spiral line, a curved line, a snowflake line, a triangle line, and the most beautiful line in the world.

6. Select your favorite lines and, using a marker, draw them horizontally across the colored paper.

7. Look at your lines and fill in any spaces with additional designs to enhance the composition.

8. Limit the number of oil crayons you use to complete the design by adding color to the spaces and shapes formed by the lines.

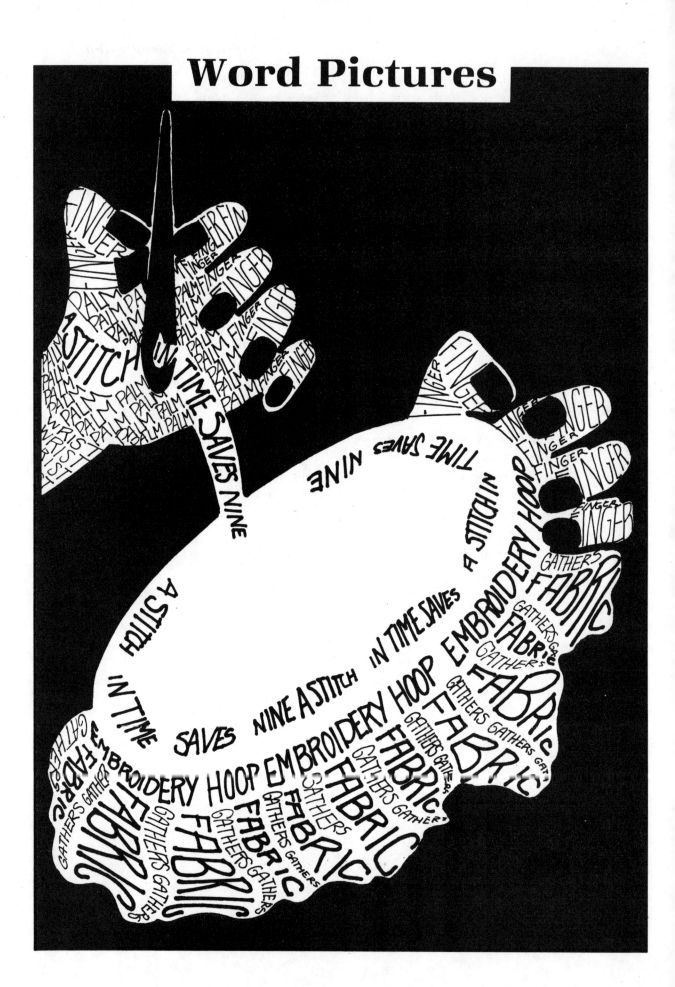

WORD PICTURES

Materials:

- 9″ × 12″ white paper
- pencil, eraser, ruler
- thick, black markers and thin, black markers
- crayons or colored markers

Directions:

1. Begin by selecting your subject matter. Ideas should not be very small or very detailed, or else they will be too difficult to fill in.

2. Once you've decided on your idea and sketched it onto white paper, you will then be ready to design your picture by selecting the words and the layout of the lettering.

3. You have many choices: You may wish to use words that identify each object or words that say something about it. See the following examples:

Don't outline your shapes with a marker. Outlines are created when a shape is filled in.

4. Within each shape there are many different directions your lettering can take.

5. Some lettering may be done with thick markers and some may be done with thin ones. Some lettering might look best large, while other lettering might look best small.

Sunglasses

SUNGLASSES

Materials:

- 12″ × 18″ oaktag
- pencil and eraser
- scissors
- thin, colored markers

Directions:

1. Draw a pair of sunglasses so that the ends reach about 2″ from each end of the paper horizontally as shown.

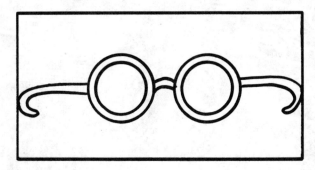

2. Draw the lenses larger than normal.
3. Cut out the glasses but leave the lenses intact.
4. In each lens, draw a scene you would like to see if you could see only one scene through your glasses, such as an underwater scene, outerspace, life on a cloud, and so forth.
5. Draw a symbol for your scene, for example, a cloud, a balloon, or a heart, and repeat it all along the frame.
6. Color in your work with the markers.

Collage Portraits

COLLAGE PORTRAITS

Materials:

- scissors
- glue
- scrap materials for collage (fabrics, yarn, leather, straw, fake fur, buttons, construction paper, wallpaper, and so forth)
- 12″ × 18″ piece of chipboard or oaktag

Directions:

1. Ask someone to model for you and observe the human head.
2. Use a ruler to check that the eyes are near the middle of the head.
3. Notice where the nose starts and ends in relation to the eyes and how close it comes to the mouth.
4. Notice the distance between the mouth and the bottom of the chin and the space between the eyes.
5. Using the collage materials, begin to cut out a large head for a portrait. Do no drawing first.
6. Cut out a neck.
7. Use other materials to add shoulders, hair, features, hats, whatever you like.
8. Make your collage portrait interesting by using a variety of materials, but select each one carefully.
9. Think of an expression for your portrait. What mood is your person in?

Costume Collage

COSTUME COLLAGE

Materials:

- sharp scissors and fabric or craft glue
- fabric of all kinds
- notions of all kinds: rick-rack, ribbon, lace, and so forth
- raffia
- yarn
- burlap
- felt
- cotton
- crayons
- pencil and eraser

Directions:

1. Think of a costume you would like to wear for Halloween.
2. Draw a simple outline of your head and body as shown. You may put yourself in an action position that your Halloween character might take.

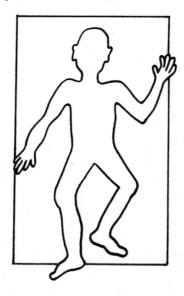

3. Cut pieces of cloth that show what your character wears and glue it to the body.
4. Glue on additional materials to help show your character more clearly.
5. Using crayons, draw in a face or add whatever else you may want in the picture.

SECTION IV ▬ ▬ **Ceramics** ▬

Level 1

Simple clay construction techniques are introduced in the lesson *Clay Candlesticks.* Working with a ball of clay, students learn to hollow out, shape, and decorate their candlesticks. In *Ceramic Coil Mirrors,* the coil method of construction is introduced along with the technique of welding. *Clay Face Necklaces* is a lesson in pushing, pulling, pinching and rolling clay in order to shape a desired surface. *Heart Frames and Necklaces* are created by using the slab technique along with cookie cutters. The cookie cutter not only creates the inner frame shape but also provides the shape for the necklace.

Heart Frames and Necklaces

Level 2

In the lesson *Clay Bells,* students begin by creating a pinch pot and then converting it to a bell. *Clay Pockets* is an introduction to simple slab construction as well as an opportunity for students to create interesting textures and patterns in clay using a variety of tools.

Clay Pockets

Level 3

Coil Pottery is a lesson that reinforces coil construction techniques while introducing their use in a three-dimensional object. In *Clay Appliqué,* students join pieces of clay together to create a relief. *Evergreen Plaques* is a lesson that makes use of natural forms to create incised designs.

Coil Pottery

Clay Candlesticks

CLAY CANDLESTICKS

Materials:

- clay
- newspaper
- pencil or carving tool
- paint and brushes

Directions:

1. Take a handful of clay and roll it into a ball. (It should be about the size of a snowball.)
2. Next, place it on top of a sheet of newspaper and push it down a little in order to flatten out the bottom.

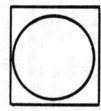 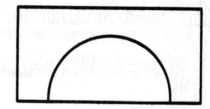

3. Now use your thumb (or a candle) to press a hole into the center of the ball.

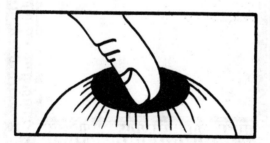

4. Using a pencil or a clay carving tool, decorate the outside with lines. You may wish to draw a picture or else just make designs.
5. After the clay has been dried thoroughly, it can be fired and then additional decoration can be done with paint.

Ceramic Coil Mirrors

CERAMIC COIL MIRRORS

Materials:

- 3" square mirror
- clay—very moist
- clay mat
- heavy paper pie plate
- 2¾" square pieces of paper
- pencil and eraser
- clay tools
- cord

Directions:

1. Practice rolling coils on your mat by first squeezing some clay in your hand into an elongated shape and then, using the palm of your hand, roll the coils out on your mat with slight pressure in a back and forth motion.

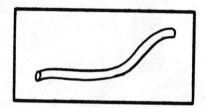

2. Trace around your square piece of paper on the inside bottom of the plate. This area will not be covered because the mirror will fit in here after the firings.

3. The side showing will be the back, and all coils have to be carefully smoothed together. Create different designs by spiraling or using different sizes of coils.

4. Dig two small holes through the frame with a clay tool. Later a cord will be strung through the holes for a hanger.

5. The plates will retain the shape of the coil frame as the clay dries.

6. Bisque, glaze, and fire again.

7. Glue the mirror to the back of the frame and string the cord through the holes.

Clay Face Necklaces

CLAY FACE NECKLACES

Materials:

- clay
- pencil or clay tool
- newspaper
- paint and brushes
- ribbon, string, or leather strip

Directions:

1. Take a handful of clay and roll it into a ball; then flatten it out on a piece of newspaper until it looks like a circle.
2. Next use your pencil or clay tool to trim the edges of your circle.
3. You can begin to form your facial features by pushing or pulling the clay to raise a nose or a forehead, or a chin and cheeks.
4. You can experiment with a pencil and "draw" directly on the clay to make outlines, or you may take extra clay and roll "snakes" to make hair or balls to make pop-out eyes.
5. Use your pencil to make a hole near the top of your clay head. You should do this because when the face is completed, a string or ribbon can be threaded through the hole so that you can wear your creation.
6. When you are done shaping your face, it should be thoroughly dried and then fired. After this process you can paint your face.

Heart Frames and Necklaces

HEART FRAMES AND NECKLACES

Materials:

- clay
- rolling pin or wood cylinder
- newspaper
- silk cord or ribbon
- clay tool or dull pencil
- square cardboard pattern
- heart-shaped cookie cutter or cardboard heart pattern
- tempera paint and brushes
- colored markers

Directions:

1. On top of a sheet of newspaper, begin by rolling your clay into a ball shape and then flattening it out with both hands.

2. Next, use a rolling pin or wood cylinder to flatten the clay out very evenly.

3. Place a square cardboard pattern on top of your clay and trace around it using a clay tool or dull pencil. Remove the excess clay from the edges.

4. Next, center your heart cookie cutter in the middle of your clay square and press just lightly enough to get an outline. You don't want to cut out the shape yet. If you are using a cardboard heart pattern the same applies. Trace around it lightly.

5. Now you are ready to decorate your frame by drawing with a tool or pencil in the areas surrounding the heart. You can make patterns or designs or even draw a scene.

6. Now you are ready to use the cookie cutter to remove the heart. After doing so, you can decorate your heart and poke a hole through it in order to be able to use it as a necklace later.

7. Both your frame and heart should be set aside to dry and then be fired.

8. After firing, hearts can be decorated with tempera paint or colored markers.

Clay Bells

CLAY BELLS

Materials:

- clay
- modeling tools, random objects to create marks in clay
- pencil
- newspaper
- pipe cleaner

Directions:

1. On top of a sheet of newspaper, roll one handful of clay into a ball the size of a snowball.

2. Now hold the ball in your left hand while you push your right thumb directly through the center of the clay ball. Be careful not to poke your thumb right through and out the other side.

3. Now start to push your thumb against the outer walls of the clay ball while pushing and flattening the outer clay wall with your remaining fingers. This will cause the original hole that your thumb made to grow larger and larger. Continue this process (turning the clay in your left hand) until you begin to have a bowl or cup shape.

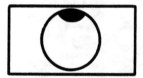 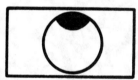  

4. Next, turn your bowl upside down and carefully poke a hole through the center of the top with a pencil.

5. Roll a small clay snake and attach it above the hole. Then use a pencil or clay tool to create a face on the front of your bell; you can add hats, hair, ears, and so forth.

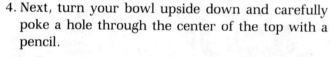

6. Make a small clay ball and poke a hole with a pencil right through the middle of it.

7. Set aside your clay pieces until they are thoroughly dry; then fire them. Fire the clay high so the sound of the bell will be good.

8. Assemble your bell by tying a knot in a length of string and "threading" it through the hole in your bead. Then bring your string through the hole in the top of your bell and tie it to the handle.

Clay Pockets

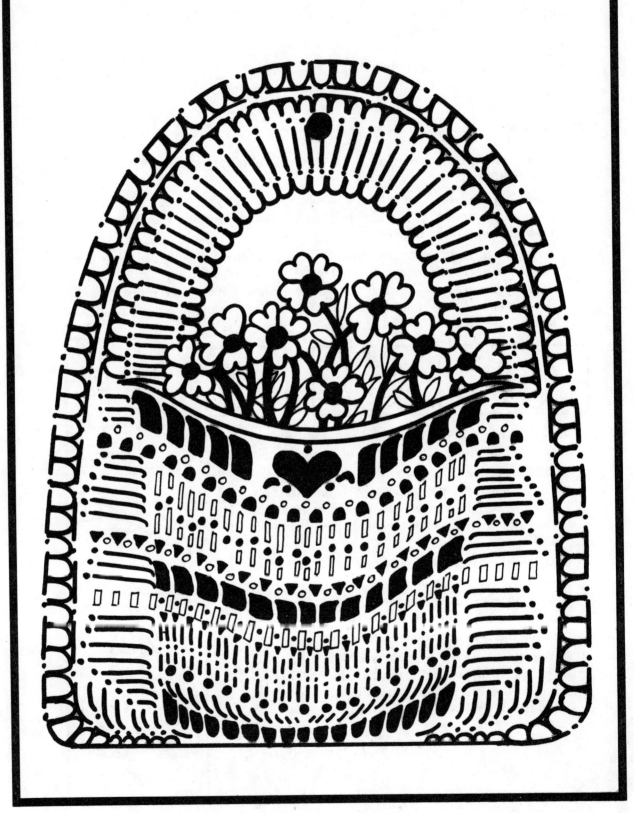

CLAY POCKETS

Materials:

- red clay for kiln firing or self-hardening clay
- oval cardboard shape
- two 10″ strips of lattice
- rolling pin
- clay modeling tools

- assorted textural objects (shells, tools for leather tooling, combs, gears, and so forth)
- mat
- cloth
- clear glaze

Directions:

1. Roll out a ball of clay between two lattice strips to ensure a uniformly thick slab.

2. Lay the oval cardboard shape on the slab and using a thin modeling tool, cut around the cardboard as if you were cutting out a giant cookie.

3. Set aside the extra clay.

4. Place the oval vertically in front of you and "twirl" the end of a modeling tool through the clay about ½″ from the top, which will enable it to be hung.

5. Gently fold the bottom part of the oval over one hand, which you should lay on the clay to form a pocket as shown. You might also stuff the cavity with newspaper, which will burn up in the firing process.

6. Using your thumb, gently press together where the edges of the clay now touch, leaving the pocket open as shown.

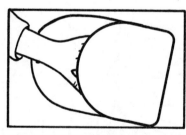

7. Leave your thumb prints as a textural interest and add more texture by using various objects previously mentioned.

8. Let the clay dry slowly by keeping it covered with a slightly damp cloth.

9. Fire and glaze or leave unglazed.

10. Dried flowers or grasses may be placed in the pocket.

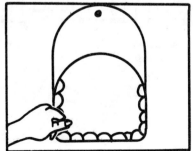

Coil Pottery

COIL POTTERY

Materials:

- clay for kiln or self-hardening clay
- plastic bowls
- thin plastic bags and ties
- mats

Directions:

1. Open a plastic bag and place it inside the plastic bowl. Make the bag conform to the shape of the inside of the bowl. Let the remainder of the plastic bag overlap its sides.

2. Take a small ball of clay and squeeze it slightly into an elongated shape like a hot dog.

3. Lay the clay on a mat and gently roll it into a coil or a "snake" using the fingers of both hands and pressing slightly as you roll together.

4. Wind this coil up to make a base for your pot as shown.

5. Smooth the top only with your fingers so that you cannot see the coils on this one side.

6. Place this coil base in the bottom of your bowl on the plastic and add whatever coils are needed to completely cover the bottom.

7. Roll shorter coils and wind them as you did with the base. Begin using these to cover the inside of the bowl, starting around the base and continuing upward as shown.

8. Continue to add more small, wound coils all the way around and above the previous rows, against the inside of the bowl until you reach the rim.

9. Gently smooth the entire inside of the bowl with your fingers.

10. Do not press too hard or you will also smooth out the coil design on the side facing the bowl.

11. Work that is stopped in progress can be preserved by gently closing the bag and sealing it with a twist tie so that no more air enters the bag.

12. When finished, leave the bag open but loosely pushed into the bowl so that it can dry slowly.

13. When thoroughly dry, remove the bag by gently pulling up on the bag and down on the plastic bowl. Then gently pull off the plastic bag.

14. Your bowl should then be allowed to dry further until it no longer feels cool against your cheek.

15. After one firing the bowl can be glazed and then fired once more.

Clay Appliqué Plaque

CLAY APPLIQUÉ PLAQUE

Materials:

- clay for kiln firing or self-hardening clay
- two 10″ lattice strips
- rolling pin
- two mats
- modeling tools
- oaktag

Directions:

1. Draw a circle or oval on oaktag that is precisely the size of the plaque you want and cut it out.
2. Roll the clay between two lattice strips with a rolling pin to achieve a slab of uniform thickness and place it on one of the mats.
3. Lay the pattern on the slab and cut around it with a thin modeling tool, as though you were cutting out a giant cookie.
4. Carefully remove any excess slab pieces and set them aside on the other mat.
5. About ½″ from the top of the plaque, twirl a tool through the clay to make a hole for hanging.
6. Using a thin modeling tool, cut desired appliqués (shapes) out of the extra slab pieces to make a picture and lay them on the plaque.
7. Using a modeling tool, gently push clay from the edges of the applied pieces downward in order to attach them to the plaque. Marks can then be smoothed out with your index finger or left as a part of the decoration.
8. Part of the picture could be drawn with incised lines using the modeling tools.
9. Let the clay dry slowly under a damp cloth so that it will not buckle.
10. Fire and glaze your plaque and shellac it.
11. A piece of yarn or ribbon can be placed through the hole to hang it.

Evergreen Plaques

EVERGREEN PLAQUES

Materials:

- oval cardboard shape
- clay for kiln firing or self-hardening clay
- two 10″ lattice strips
- rolling pin
- clay modeling tools
- piece of evergreen
- mat
- glaze or tempera and shellac
- cloth
- green printing ink

Directions:

1. Roll out a ball of clay between two lattice strips to ensure a uniformly thick slab.
2. Lay the oval cardboard shape on the slab and, using a thin modeling tool, cut around the cardboard as if you were cutting out a giant cookie.
3. Set aside the extra clay.
4. Place a piece of evergreen on the clay and lightly roll the rolling pin over it until an impression has been made in the clay.
5. Gently pull out the evergreen piece and let the clay dry slowly with a damp cloth over it.
6. When dry, fire the plaque and glaze or paint it as desired.
7. An alternate method for finishing is to wipe green printing ink over the plaque after firing, and then to keep wiping it with a damp cloth until the pine impression has absorbed most of the ink and the remainder of the surface is a light tint.
8. Let dry and shellac.

Level 1

In the first activity, *Torn Paper Trees,* small torn paper shapes are arranged to create a mosaic-like tree with brightly colored leaves. *Paper Bag Houses* are three-dimensional constructions that employ a variety of simple paper sculpture techniques. The lesson *Stitched Paper Puppets* introduces puppetry, as well as simple sewing, as a technique for joining pieces of paper. The craft of paper quilling is introduced and explored in the next activity, *Quilling Valentines.*

Stitched Paper Puppets

Level 2

Paper Sculpture Animals are created by using a wide variety of paper sculpture techniques. Students are encouraged to bend, fold, roll, crumple, crimp, curl, or pleat in order to create their animals. In the next lesson, paper *Witches* come alive when their paper parts are assembled and then joined with brass fasteners. In *Oaktag Houses,* basic architectural concepts are introduced and then put into practice as students create a three-dimensional building using stiff paper. Kite making is introduced and the unique qualities of tissue paper explored in the lesson *Tissue Paper Fish Kites. Two-Cardboard Relief* is an introduction to relief that uses cardboard layers to build up the varying surface levels in the composition. *Dancing Bears* are simple, fun paper toys that come to life when students learn to "let their fingers do the walking" for these ballroom bears.

Oaktag Houses

Level 3

Landscape in the Round is a lesson that explores the spatial relationships that exist between the different elements in a landscape. The next activity, *Lunar Shadow Box,* is one that stresses imagination and inventiveness as students create a unique environment using primarily found objects and scrap materials. *Paper Bag People* are characters that are created by stuffing, shaping, stapling, and painting various paper bags. The silhouette is introduced and used as an overlay on a tissue paper collage background in the lesson *Tissue Paper Silhouettes.*

Tissue Paper Silhouettes

Torn Paper Trees

TORN PAPER TREES

Materials:

- 12″ × 18″ blue paper
- glue or paste
- scraps of paper: brown, orange, yellow, green

Directions:

1. Imagine how a tree grows: The roots take hold in the ground, the trunk thickens, and branches divide from it; they then divide again and get thinner until they are the tiny twigs on the ends of the branches. Leaves come out and then begin to fall in the autumn.
2. Tear out a big, wide trunk for your "tree" out of the brown scrap paper.
3. You will have an easier time if you tear the paper slowly with little movements of your fingers.
4. Glue the trunk on your blue paper.
5. Tear out a few big branches to extend off the trunk and glue these on your paper.
6. Tear out thinner, shorter branches or twigs and glue these so that they extend off the few big branches.
7. Tear some leaves out of the remaining colors and glue some of them on the branches and some on the ground to show ones that have fallen.

Paper Bag Houses

PAPER BAG HOUSES

Materials:

- lunch bag
- assorted colored paper
- markers or paint
- cardboard
- white glue

Directions:

1. Lay a lunch bag in front of you, still flat, with the top of the bag pointing away from you.
2. Add features such as doors, windows, shutters, and chimneys by using white glue and pieces of colored paper.
3. Open up the bag and stuff it with two single sheets of crumpled newspaper.
4. Fold the top over once or twice and staple, taking care to make sure the bag retains a box-like shape.
5. Fold one sheet of construction paper in half and staple over the top of the bag to create the roof.

 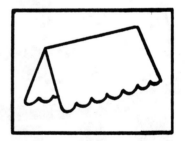

6. Cardboard may be glued to the base of the house to allow room for trees, fences, mailboxes, people, and cars.
7. Additional details can be added with markers.

Stitched Paper Puppets

STITCHED PAPER PUPPETS

Materials:

- 2 pieces of brown butcher paper, 12″ × 18″
- tempera and brushes
- yarn and yarn needles
- pencil and eraser

Directions:

1. Lay your hand and part of your arm on one piece of paper.

2. Around this draw a large character for your puppet. Draw it as large as possible on the paper.
3. Possible characters might be clowns, baseball players, a princess, and so forth.
4. Remove your arm and add features and details.
5. Cut out and place on a second piece of paper.
6. Trace around except for the feet.
7. Paint with bold, bright colors.
8. Let dry.
9. Stitch using an overlapping stitch front to back with yarn. Leave a large opening at the puppet's feet.

Quilling Valentines

QUILLING VALENTINES

Materials:

- 3 doilies
- 2 sheets of red construction paper
- thin strips of white paper
- white glue
- scissors and pencil

Directions:

1. Arrange three medium-sized doilies on a sheet of 9″ × 12″ red construction paper so that they overlap like this. Then glue them in place.

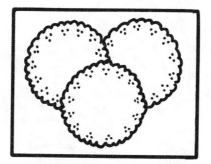

2. Next, fold your other 9″ × 12″ sheet of red construction paper in half and draw half of a heart starting at the fold as shown.

3. Cut it out, center it on top of your doilies and then glue it in place.

4. Next, take a thin, white strip of paper and roll it up around a pencil or crayon. Then, slide it off the pencil (but don't let it uncurl yet) and dip it into a puddle of white glue. (Your "puddle" should be in a plastic lid or on top of scrap cardboard.) Next, place it along the outline of your heart and let it uncurl a little as you hold it in place to dry.

5. Continue to make and add spirals until your heart is full.

Paper Sculpture Animals

PAPER SCULPTURE ANIMALS

Materials:

- 9″ × 12″ white and colored construction paper
- scissors
- glue
- stapler, masking tape

A **mural** is a large artwork hung or made directly on a wall. A mural can be made of a variety of materials such as paint, chalk, paper, wood, and so forth. Usually a theme is chosen, such as a zoo, a circus, the classroom, a city, a farm, a jungle, an undersea world. This offers the opportunity to explore composition on a larger scale. In museums you can see examples of Greek, Egyptian, and Chinese murals. Early man drew murals of animals and hunting scenes on the walls of his caves.

Directions:

1. Think of your favorite zoo animal: an elephant, a giraffe, a bear, a monkey.
2. Think about the appearance of each animal: the long legs and long neck of the giraffe, a squirrel's bushy tail, a camel's hump, an elephant's long trunk, and a kangaroo's strong hind legs.
3. Flat paper has two directions or dimensions: width and length. A three-dimensional object has another direction: depth or thickness.
4. You can make a flat piece of paper stand by itself. You can fold it, curve it, or roll it and fasten it to make a cylinder. It can also be crumpled to make it stand.
5. You can run the paper over the blade of a scissors or roll the paper around a pencil to make it curl.
6. Try cutting a line into the center of a paper and then overlapping the edges. This will mound the paper up into a cone.
7. Try folding a piece of paper these ways: into hinges, into box-like shapes, into reverse pleats, folding two strips of paper over and over each other to make a spring-like object.
8. Try crumpling a piece of paper. It can be left as a ball, or it can be opened again into an almost flat, bumpy paper.
9. Don't use any pencils or make drawings first. Don't add any details with pencil or crayon. If the parts are too small to cut from the paper, they are too small to show.
10. Decide what kind of an animal you would like to make, and then choose your paper.
11. Be sure you make the animal strong enough to stand. Make his legs the same length so that he can stand easily. Make sure your animal balances to stand alone.
12. Make several animals for your zoo.

Witches

WITCHES

Materials:

- pencil and eraser
- green, black, brown construction paper
- scissors

- glue
- 4 brass fasteners
- thin, black marker

Directions:

1. Draw and cut out the profile (side view of a person's face and nose where you see only one eye) of a witch's face on green paper. Make her have a pointed chin, a crooked nose, and a narrow, wicked eye. Be sure to include a neck.

2. Draw and cut out a crooked witch's hat and stringy hair and glue them onto the head of the witch.

3. Draw and cut out a ragged dress shape on black paper—as shown—with an opening for the neck.

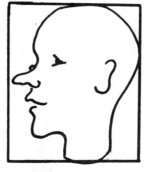

4. Glue the neck underneath the dress opening.

5. To make each arm for your witch use green paper to draw the two separate shapes, as shown, and cut them out. One shape is the upper arm and the other is the lower arm and hand. See the illustration below.

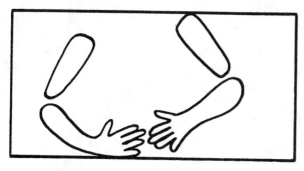
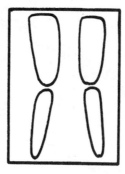

6. Glue the top of the arm parts under the sleeve openings.

7. On green paper, draw one pair of the two leg parts, as shown, for the thigh area and the calf area.

8. Glue the tops of the leg parts under the dress opening.

9. Attach the tops and bottoms of the arms and legs together with a brass fastener, which you push through both pieces. Spread the "wings" of the fasteners to hold them in place. Overlap the leg parts slightly at the knees and the arm parts at the elbows to enable your witch to bend just as we do.

10. Cut out shoes and glue them on the legs.

11. Cut and glue an object for your witch to hold, such as a broom, a cat, a pumpkin, and so forth.

Oaktag Houses

OAKTAG HOUSES

Materials:

- oaktag
- 9″ × 12″ heavy cardboard
- scissors and glue
- popsicle sticks and cotton swabs

Directions:

1. Ask yourself if you would rather be in a tent or a glass house, a cozy tree house or a soft, warm, sunny field.
2. These are all very different spaces, and you would feel differently living in each.
3. Look at pictures or slides of a variety of buildings and architecture. As you view the pictures, ask yourself which buildings look strong, and which look light and airy.
4. Using the oaktag, sticks, and swabs, make a shelter that has a feeling of openness.
5. To make it easier to glue corners, you should draw and cut each so that each has a fold to overlap and glue together.
6. To make folding easier, hold a ruler on the dotted line and fold over, or either run or score a single blade of the scissors on the dotted line of the fold.
7. Cut out windows and doors before gluing them on the cardboard base.

Tissue Paper Fish Kites

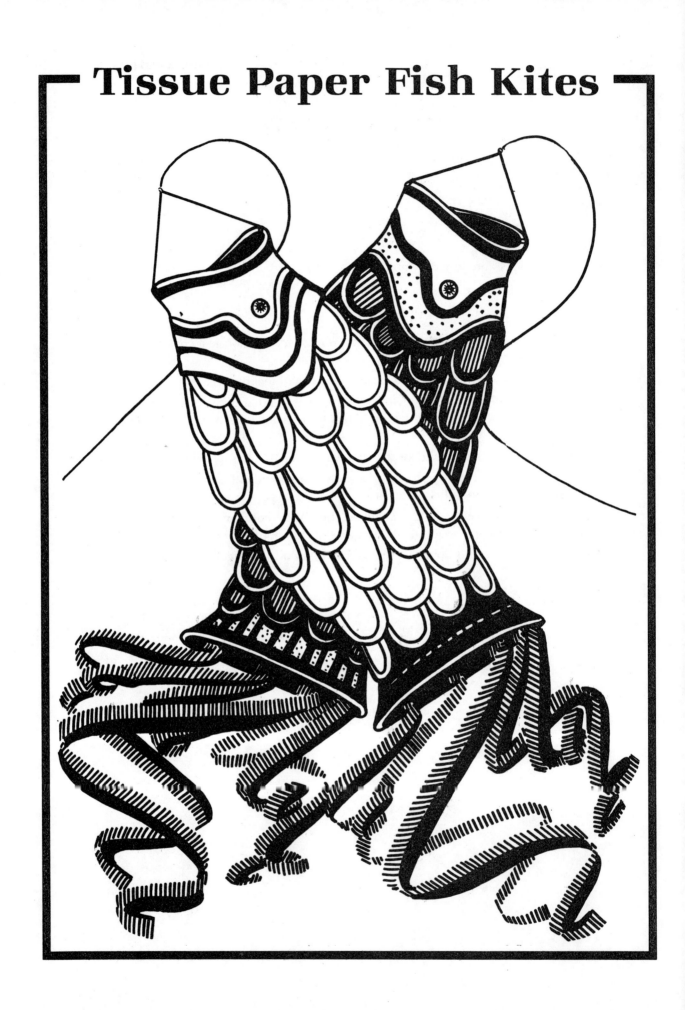

TISSUE PAPER FISH KITES

Materials:

- tissue paper and construction paper
- white glue
- pipe cleaner
- string

Directions:

1. On one large, folded sheet of construction paper, draw your fish making sure that the tail touches one end of the paper and that the mouth touches the other end. Keep your outline simple. Extend the length of the mouth, because this will later be folded back.

2. Cut out your fish and place it on top of two sheets of tissue paper. Trace around the fish with a marker and cut through both sheets on the outline.

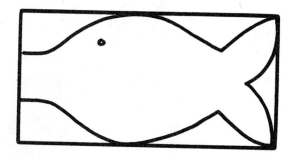

3. Use additional tissue paper to cut out fish scales. Attach these with white glue to each side of your fish and then glue the two sides together. Do not glue the tail or mouth closed so that the wind can pass through the kite when flown.

 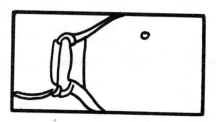

4. Fold back the mouth and slide a pipe cleaner through the fold; twist it closed and glue down the fold with white glue. Bend the pipe cleaner a bit to open the mouth; attach a piece of string.

5. Cut long, thin strips of tissue paper and attach these with white glue to the tail.

Two-Cardboard Relief

TWO-CARDBOARD RELIEF

Materials:

- 12″ × 18″ heavy cardboard
- thin shirt cardboard or the inside of a corrugated cardboard shoe box top for a simple picture which also provides a frame
- scissors and glue
- pencil and eraser

Directions:

1. Relief is a picture or design made up of surfaces that are raised from the background by the thickness of one or more layers.
2. Think of a scene where exciting action is taking place: a fire in a high-rise, an elephant stampede in the jungle, two dinosaurs in fierce combat, and so forth.
3. Begin to cut out the larger objects or shapes needed for your picture and glue them on the heavy cardboard.
4. Continue with medium-size shapes and then small ones.
5. Check to see that your space is filled properly and that you have fully told your exciting story by including enough objects, people, or animals.
6. Is the weather an important factor to consider in order to heighten the excitement of your picture?
7. In some places, have smaller pieces of cardboard on top of others to create more of a relief effect.
8. Paint all cardboard shapes with tempera and let dry.

Dancing Bears

DANCING BEARS

Materials:

- oaktag, posterboard, or light cardboard
- crayons or markers
- pencils, scissors
- glue
- felt

Directions:

1. Begin by outlining your bear on a piece of oaktag approximately 4″ × 6″. You can lay out your bear by using a series of circles. See the following illustration. Note that you are not drawing legs on the bear.

2. Next, outline the arms and add clothes: a bow tie and top hat or perhaps a tutu and crown. Then draw two circles in the space where the legs would begin. See the illustration on the right.

3. Now, use markers or crayons to color and decorate your bear. When this is done, cut out the bear and poke a hole into each of the leg circles and cut those out as well.

4. Insert your index and middle finger through the holes and your bear is ready to "dance."

Landscape in the Round

LANDSCAPE IN THE ROUND

Materials:

- oaktag
- stapler
- scissors
- markers
- colored construction paper

Directions:

1. You are going to build a landscape—any scene outdoors—right here.
2. Four things will be needed: (1) the baseline (ground or water); (2) objects at, below, or slightly above this line; (3) objects in the sky; and (4) space.
3. Objects cannot float in space by themselves (except in outer space), away from gravity, or in water (where they need the water in order to float).
4. Objects must be related to each other: boats and fish need water, houses and volcanoes need land. Clouds, the sun, planes, and parachutists somewhere must touch objects that project from a baseline in order to express their relationship to them.
5. In our real world, clouds, stars, and a rising sun at the horizon are intruded upon by hills, houses, and trees.
6. Overlapping oaktag shapes will capture this arrangement.
7. Don't arrange the landscape flat on a table because you will not be able to see the spaces between the objects. These spaces are important, so do your arranging by holding your landscape up and away from you.
8. Begin by cutting a piece of oaktag 18″ × 3″. Circle this around and staple so that it will sit on a table.
9. This will be your ground or water.
10. Build from here and/or on this piece.
11. Space is captured between objects by joining sky objects in an over-arching pattern, like an umbrella.
12. At least two sky objects must touch opposite land or sea areas for balance.
13. Did you include vehicles or people in your landscape?

Lunar Shadow Boxes

LUNAR SHADOW BOXES

Materials:

- shoe box
- colored cellophane
- tape
- glue and scissors
- cotton
- scrap materials of all kinds: wood, fabric, notions, yarn, boxes, string, and so forth

Directions:

1. Turn a shoe box on its side and think of the inside as the dark side of the moon—the side no one has seen. Do you think anything lives there? What kind of objects make up a "moonscape"?

2. You may want to suspend objects on strings or build objects on the bottom. What do you think the surface would be like?

3. Creatures, buildings, animals, or vehicles may be added.

4. When the inside is finished, cover the front with a light-colored cellophane that has been cut a little larger than the opening and glued to the sides.

Paper Bag People

PAPER BAG PEOPLE

Materials:

- paper lunch bags
- stapler
- newspaper
- paper and cardboard
- tempera and brushes
- starch

- cloth
- colored tissue paper
- black markers
- gloss acrylic polymer
- yarn
- glue and scissors

Directions:

1. Stuff the bags with crushed and torn newspaper. Whole or parts of bags can be used.
2. Staple bags together as has been done in the figure shown.
3. Staple on cardboard hands and feet as shown.

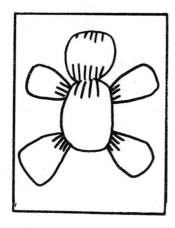 

4. Glue on additional paper parts such as eyes, nose, and mouth, hats, and paper curls, or use yarn for hair.
5. Paint with tempera mixed with starch.
6. Use cloth or colored tissue for clothing.

Tissue Paper Silhouettes

TISSUE PAPER SILHOUETTES

Materials:

- assorted pastel colors of tissue paper
- tissue collage glue or watered down white glue
- 1 sheet white paper, 12″ × 18″
- 1 sheet black paper, 9″ × 12″
- pencils, scissors
- glue brushes
- manila practice paper

Directions:

1. To begin, tear interesting shapes from different pastel colored sheets of tissue paper.

2. Arrange these shapes on your white paper. Move the shapes around until you find a pleasing arrangement. Perhaps a collection of shapes will start to look like something you recognize: a wave, a mountain, a sunset, a forest. If it does, you may want to tear additional shapes more deliberately so that you can control the scene you are creating. You do not *have* to create a scene because in these pictures a random design will also work nicely.

3. Brush the glue over the tissue paper to keep the shapes in place. Fill up every bit of your paper. When you get to the edges of your paper you can let the tissue overhang and trim this excess off later when it's dry.

4. After filling your entire paper with shapes put it aside to dry.

5. While you are waiting you can begin to sketch your silhouettes. You may wish to make some practice sketches on manila paper to see what kinds of things make good silhouettes. Remember that silhouettes rely on the details provided in their outlines to show what they are.

6. Once you've decided, draw your silhouette on black paper, cut it out, and use glue to attach it to your tissue paper background.

SECTION VI — **Printmaking**

Level 1

The first activity in this chapter, *Handprints,* is a lesson in the simplest form of printmaking. Students produce a print of their hand by making a direct impression of it in clay. The concept of texture, both visual and tactile, is introduced in *Texture Prints.* Printmaking from a stencil is introduced in the lesson *Chalk Prints.*

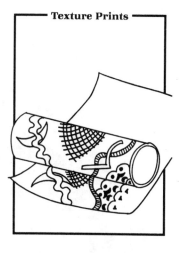

Texture Prints

Level 2

Two-Color Styrofoam Prints is an activity that introduces two-color printmaking with the use of negative and positive space. *Tempera Tile Prints* provides an introduction to the printing brayer as well as to the use of found objects in creating a pressed print. *Leaf Prints* provides further exploration of the incised print as well as an opportunity to work directly from nature.

Two-Color Styrofoam Prints

Level 3

Gadget Prints reinforces the use of found objects in printmaking as well as the process of pressed prints.

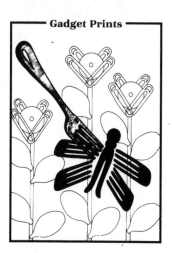

Gadget Prints

Handprints

WHITNEY

HANDPRINTS

Materials:

- clay
- newspaper
- rolling pin or wood cylinder
- clay tool or dull pencil
- cardboard circle
- spray paint or tempera paint and polymer

Directions:

1. Handprints are one of the simplest forms of printmaking. Captured in clay, they will last forever.

2. Begin by rolling your clay into the shape of a large ball. Next, place it on top of some newspaper and begin to flatten out the ball by pushing down on it with both hands.

3. Next, use a rolling pin to flatten it out evenly.

4. Place a cardboard circle (large enough to fit your hand) on top of the clay and trace around it with a clay tool or a dull pencil. Remove the extra clay from the edges.

5. Now you are ready to print by simply placing your right hand in the center of your clay circle and pressing down on it with your left hand to get a clear impression.

6. You may wish to write your name and date on the plaque and create designs all around the edge with a clay tool or dull pencil.

7. Using your pencil, make a hole near the top of your plaque; then set it aside to dry.

8. After firing, plaques can be spray painted or painted with tempera and then coated with polymer. A ribbon can be looped through the hole in the top of the plaque and tied in a bow if so desired.

Texture Prints

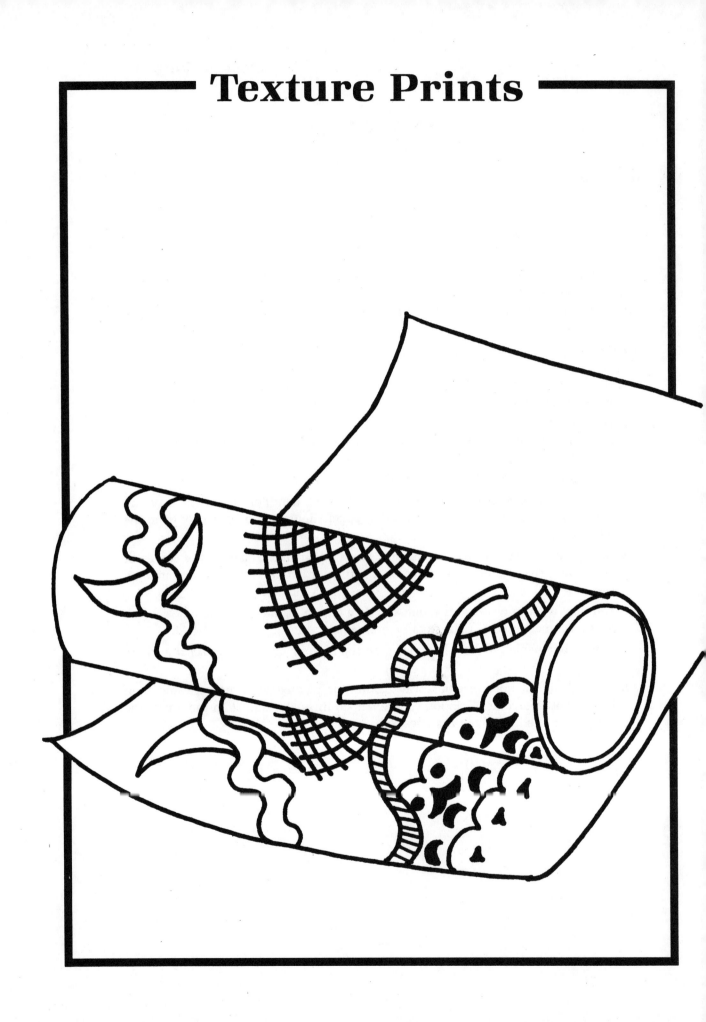

TEXTURE PRINTS

Materials:

- cardboard tube from toilet paper or paper towel roll
- scissors and glue
- scrap flat materials that have a texture or design: fabric, rickrack, ribbon, felt, burlap, trims, paper straws, pipe cleaners, yarn, doilies, wallpaper with raised designs, corrugated cardboard, and so forth
- water-based printing ink
- brayers
- tray or cookie sheet to roll out ink
- various printing papers

Directions:

1. **Select items which have an interesting texture.**
2. Glue pieces of the items all around the cardboard tube. Be sure to glue the pieces **completely flat and securely.**
3. Let dry completely.
4. Roll out ink on your tray.
5. Either roll the cardboard tube on a tray or use a brayer to roll ink onto the tube until its surface is well inked. Work quickly before the ink dries.
6. Slowly roll the tube on a piece of printing paper using your fingers inside the tube to print the various designs onto the paper. A broom handle or large dowel may be placed inside the tube when rolling to provide more pressure.
7. Let dry.

Chalk Prints

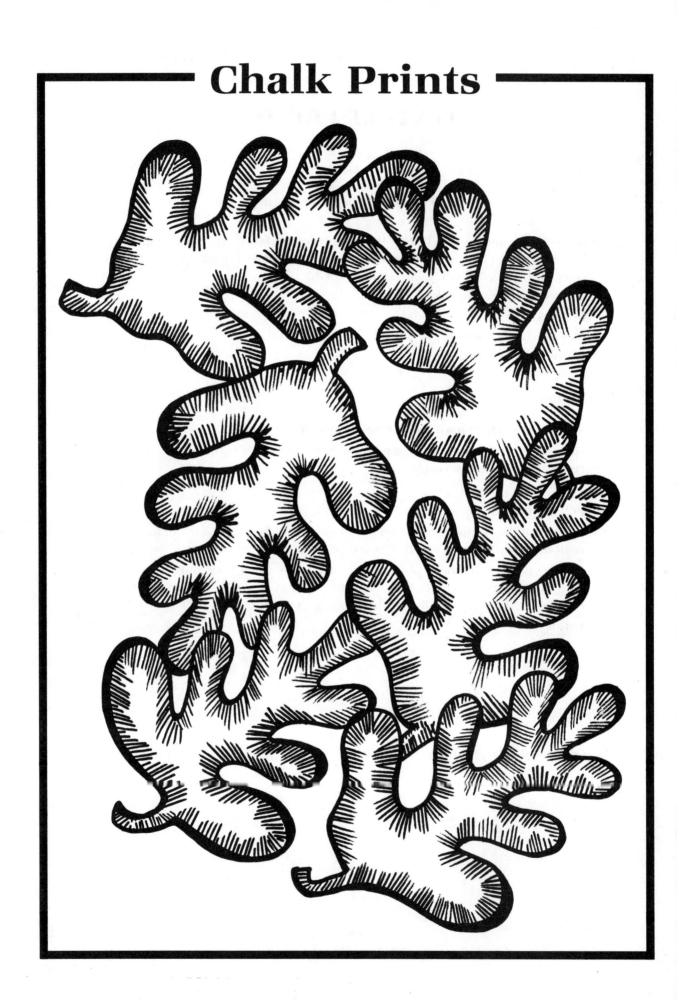

CHALK PRINTS

Materials:

- oaktag or lightweight cardboard
- colored chalk
- tissues
- construction paper
- pencils
- scissors
- newspaper

Directions:

1. The first thing you must do is make a stencil. To do this you must decide upon an idea for your picture because your stencil will be a shape that is repeated many times in your picture.
2. Once you've decided, draw your shape on a piece of oaktag.
3. Next, you must poke a hole through the middle of your shape using one blade of your scissors so that you can cut to the edges of your outline.

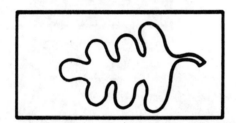

4. Next, place your stencil on top of a piece of newspaper while you color with chalk near the edges of your shape.

5. Now you are ready to place your stencil on top of your construction paper (with the chalked side up) and take a tissue so that you can rub the chalk off the oaktag into the cutout space, thereby making a print.
6. Repeat this process again and again to create your picture. Rechalk your stencil as necessary.
7. Notice what interesting things happen when you overlap your prints.

Two-Color Styrofoam Prints

TWO-COLOR STYROFOAM PRINTS

Materials:

- washed styrofoam meat trays
- water soluble printing ink in contrasting colors
- plastic trays for rolling ink
- brayers
- printing paper
- newspapers
- scissors

Directions:

1. Animals use camouflage for survival. Camouflage in nature uses color and pattern on an animal's skin, fur, or feathers to enable it to blend into its environment. By blending in, the animal cannot be seen as easily by other animals or by man.
2. Obvious examples include a leopard, snakes, a tiger, and birds.
3. Trim the edges off the tray so you can work with a flat surface.
4. Use one point of the scissors and carefully draw an environment in the soft styrofoam.
5. Use a brayer to roll the printing ink onto the styrofoam tray.
6. Place a piece of paper on top of the inked tray, and roll a clean brayer along the paper, or rub the paper with the pads of your fingers.
7. Carefully lift the inked tray off the paper.
8. Allow the print to dry.
9. Trim the edges off a second tray.
10. Draw the animal that lives in the already-printed environment and completely cut it out.
11. Repeat the inking procedure.
12. Place the inked animal on top of the dried environment print.
13. By gently pressing, the animal will become imprinted on the previous print.

Tempera Tile Prints

TEMPERA TILE PRINTS

Materials:

- tempera
- acrylic gloss medium
- 1/16″ thick pieces of poster or illustration board
- hard and soft brayers
- plastic trays to roll paint
- found objects for printing
- brush to roll tempera

Directions:

1. Roll the brayer over one tempera paint color in the plastic tray and roll in successive layers on a piece of illustration board.
2. Roll different colors, one over the other.
3. Pick found objects to print with.
4. Paint tempera on the part of the found object which has a textured surface and print over the brayer layers previously done. One object may be used in repetition as an all-over pattern or several objects may be combined in a controlled design.
5. Let dry.
6. Paint a coat of acrylic gloss medium over the ink. Smooth out any brush strokes. You may find that you want to thin this medium with a little water.

Leaf Prints

LEAF PRINTS

Materials:

- assorted green leaves (leaves should be fresh and supple)
- 9″ × 12″ newsprint paper
- scissors and glue
- black water-based printing ink
- brayer
- shallow pan or cookie sheet
- 12″ × 18″ piece of colored construction paper
- magazine

Directions:

1. Open a magazine and lay a leaf with the veined side (usually also the lighter side) up.
2. Roll ink in the pan and, holding the stem of the leaf, gently roll the ink from the stem outward at different angles.
3. Do not try to cover the entire leaf with ink. Rather, try to be able to see the network of veins as this will add an interesting pattern to your print.
4. Remove the leaf and place it ink side up on the next magazine page.
5. Lay the piece of newsprint on top of the leaf and gently rub. You will feel the veins and begin to see a faint impression of the leaf through the paper.
6. Gently peel the paper from the leaf and let the print dry.

Gadget Prints

GADGET PRINTS

Materials:

- kitchen or household gadgets, such as can openers, graters, forks, egg beaters, bottle stoppers, pizza cutters, potato mashers, corks, spools, clothespins, bottle tops, corkscrews, spatulas, and so forth
- tempera and small brushes
- 12″ × 18″ colored construction paper

Directions:

1. Brush paint on a side of an object that has an interesting shape for a print.
2. Press the object on a piece of paper to produce a print.
3. Repeat the above with other objects and paint colors.
4. You could try making a design or a picture from the objects.

 # Weaving

Level 1

The first activity in this chapter, *Straight Weaving*, introduces the concept of weaving and the basic techniques involved in this craft. New vocabulary is introduced as students learn the meaning of loom, warp, weft, and weave. The characteristics of different types of yarn are considered as students select and combine them in their work.

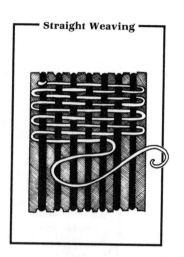

Straight Weaving

Level 2

The next activity, *Circle Weaving*, reinforces basic weaving techniques while introducing a new type of loom. Further attention is placed on the selection and placement of different types of yarn in order to create contrast and patterns in their work.

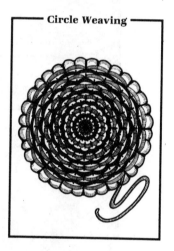

Circle Weaving

Level 3

The technique of weaving without a loom is introduced in the lesson *Paper Weaving.* In this lesson, students weave together large pieces of construction paper and the result is a large paper heart. In the lesson *Straw Weaving,* a new and unique type of loom, comprised of straws, is introduced. A weaving variation is explored in the next activity, *Ojos de Dios.* It involves the creation of designs and patterns in yarn as it is wound around wooden spokes.

Paper Weaving

Straight Weaving

STRAIGHT WEAVING

Materials:

- 6″ × 8″ piece of cardboard or styrofoam meat tray (If sytrofoam is used, place a strip of masking tape at each short end before cutting notches.)
- scissors
- skein of yarn
- scrap yarn
- pencil and eraser
- simple ruler (inches only)
- masking tape
- stick or branch slightly wider than the cardboard

Weaving is the intertwining of materials. Materials used include yarn, cord, grasses, ribbon, and so forth. Weaving can be done to produce a useful article or an artwork. A design or pattern can be planned, or the work can be spontaneous and random. Weaving has been done for thousands of years. In museums we can see examples of Egyptian, South American, Indian, and Polynesian weavings. In colonial America, cloth was woven for clothes, draperies, and coverlets.

Directions:

1. Using the ruler, mark one-inch notches about a half-inch in length across both of the six-inch ends of the cardboard or styrofoam as shown.

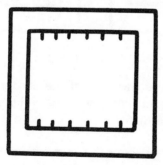

2. Take the end of the yarn on a skein and tape it to the back of the cardboard just below one of the first notches.

3. Run this through the notch to the front side.

4. Continue the yarn strand directly across to the next notch. Go through that notch, around the back of the notch immediately next to it and back through that notch to the front again.

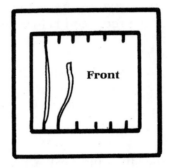

5. Continue the strand of yarn directly across to the next notch, around to the back and through the next notch all the way across the cardboard until you run out of notches. Tape the yarn strand on the back and cut.

6. Your weaving should look like this:

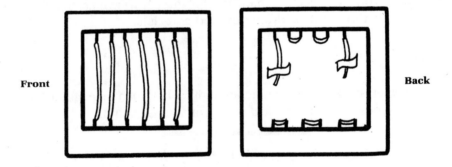

7. Cut a length of another color or type of yarn (no longer than two feet).

8. Tape one end of this yarn to the back of the cardboard as shown in "A." Bring the other end of the yarn around to the front and begin weaving over and under each yarn strand as shown in "B."

9. Take the same strand of yarn and weave back the opposite way, going over a strand you went under before and under a strand you went over before as shown below.

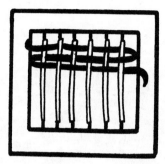

10. Continue weaving each new row, alternating the "over-under" pattern each time.

11. When you run out of a color, simply start with the new strand exactly where you ended the old, continuing the over-under pattern.

12. Push each row up against the next but *do not* pull each strand tight after each line of weaving. If you do pull each strand of weaving, your weaving will look curved like this instead of straight.

13. When you can no longer weave any more strands of yarn through, undo the tape and discard it. Pull the loops of yarn gently out of their notches and tie any ends of yarn to the nearest loop.

14. Weave a stick or branch through the top loops of the weaving and hang as a wall hanging.

Circle Weaving

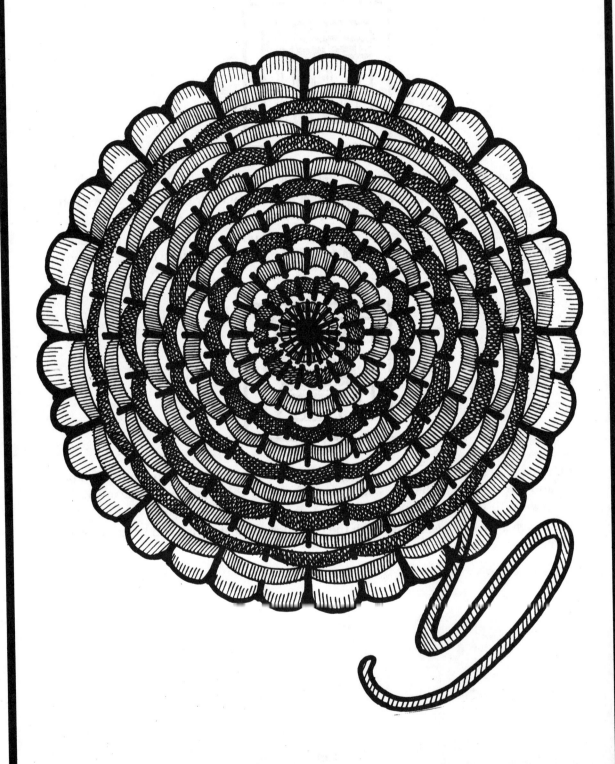

CIRCLE WEAVING

Materials:

- cardboard (pulp paper plates may also be used)
- scissors
- pencil and eraser
- yarn
- ballpoint pen
- compass
- ruler
- measuring tape
- masking tape

Directions:

1. Draw an 8″ circle on your cardboard and cut it out to make a loom.
2. Using a measuring tape, mark lines that are 1/2″ long and that are 1/2″ apart all around the edge of the circle until you have 43 lines, as shown.

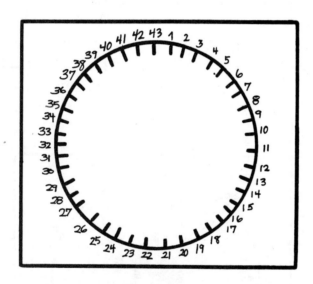

3. Cut the notches and label each with your pen from number 1 to number 43.
4. Tie a large knot in the end of a piece of yarn on a skein of yarn.
5. Do not cut the yarn.
6. Pull the end of a piece of yarn through notch number 1 so that it is in the back of the cardboard circle.
7. On the front of the circle, stretch the yarn tautly across the surface and pull it into notch number 22.
8. Wrap the yarn around the back of the circle and back through notch number 23 to the front of the circle.

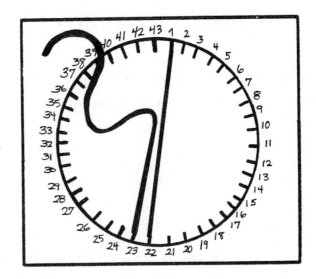

9. Continue this procedure according to the pattern of numbers shown so that the yarn stretches only across the surface of the cardboard on the front and so that the loops around the notches are only on the back.

1 – 22 – 23 – 2 – 3 – 24 – 25 – 4 – 5 – 26 – 27 – 6 – 7 – 28 –
29 – 8 – 9 – 30 – 31 – 10 – 11 – 32 – 33 – 12 – 13 – 34 – 35 –
14 – 15 – 36 – 37 – 16 – 17 – 38 – 39 – 18 – 19 – 40 – 41 – 20 –
21 – 42 – 43

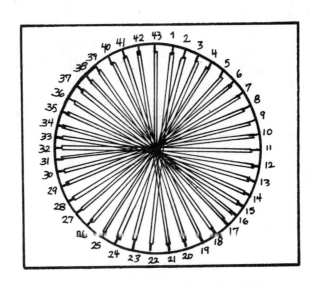

10. When you reach notch number 43, extend the yarn to the back of the circle and tape it in place with masking tape.

11. Thread a one-foot piece of yarn under the middle of your yarn design and tie in a double knot.

12. Take the other end and begin weaving at any point over and under the warp thread, pulling the yarn toward the center of your design. Continue in the same direction around the circle.

13. When this yarn runs out, tie another color or textured piece of yarn to this and continue weaving.

14. After you reach the edge of the circle, gently pull the yarn out of the notches and remove the masking tape from the end piece of the back.

15. Weave this piece into the weaving to become part of your design.

16. You may stretch the weaving out into the loops or attach fringe to each loop.

Paper Weaving

PAPER WEAVING

Materials:

- two sheets of 12″ × 18″ construction paper: one red, one white
- glue or paste
- scissors
- pencil
- ruler

Directions:

1. Place one sheet of construction paper on top of the other and draw a line where they overlap.

2. Using this line as a base, draw a half circle which touches the top of your paper. Cut along the arc of your circle, and then use this cutout as a guide for creating the same shape on the other sheet of paper.

3. Using a ruler or a 1″ strip as your guide, draw lines to divide the space below your baseline into equal strips; then cut along the lines. You can save time on this step by cutting through two sheets at once.

4. Now overlap strips as shown and begin to weave one into the other, one at a time.

5. After all the strips have been woven, the ends should be glued together on both sides.

Ojos de Dios

OJOS DE DIOS

Materials:

- yarn, colored string
- toothpicks, popsicle sticks, twigs, branches
- scissors

Directions:

1. Otherwise known as "God's Eyes," Ojos de Dios may be traced to the Indians of Mexico. They carried two shields, one in back and one in front, which were circular with a hole in the center to serve as the eye in a mask. They were thought of as representing a part of a god. Each pattern of colors was symbolic for a certain god.

2. Cross whichever two sticks you choose and wrap a few times with the string or yarn.

 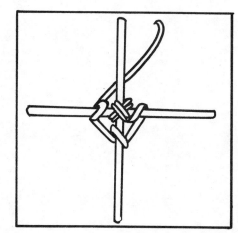

3. Then always in the same direction of rotation, the string should be brought around one stick, jumped to the next, wrapped around it, jumped to the next, and so on.

4. Change colors frequently.

5. Using three or four sticks that intersect in the center will make more complex patterns for older students.

6. It is also possible to make three-dimensional examples by inserting a stick at right angles to the basic plane with the weaving alternating between two planes.

7. For clusters of ojos built on a small branch, short sections of similar twigs may be tied in at right angles here and there to begin each "eye." Suspending other twig ojos from the branch by threads is effective.

Straw Weaving

STRAW WEAVING

Materials:

- 3 plastic drinking straws
- scissors
- yarn, ribbon
- beads or shells with a hole cut in each

Directions:

1. Cut the straws in half and keep five of the halves.
2. Cut five pieces of yarn that are each four feet long.
3. Thread each warp thread separately through each straw, out the top, and overlap about 1/2″ of it to the outside of the straw. Use a small piece of masking tape to smoothly wrap around and secure the yarn to the straw as shown. These are the warp threads.

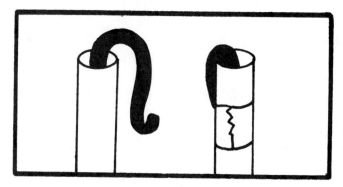

4. Make sure the tape is smooth, because rough edges will catch the yarn when you begin weaving.
5. Cut another piece of yarn about two feet long. Tie it to an end straw near the top and, holding the yarn in one hand and the five straws close together in the other, begin to pull it in and out of each straw near the top, weaving over one straw and under the next as shown. This will form the weft threads.

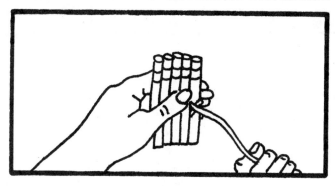

6. When you reach the end, loop the yarn around and weave back to where you began the same way: over one straw and under one as shown. Repeat.

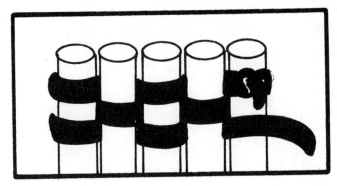

7. When you finish with this piece of yarn, tie it to another piece of yarn and continue.

8. Beads or shells can be threaded through your piece of weaving yarn at any point and can then be woven right into your belt.

9. As the tops of your straws fill up with weaving, you will need to gently push some of the weaving downward, but never let all of the weaving slip off the straws or there will be a gap in your weaving and it will be difficult to start again.

10. If you are making a belt, when it is long enough to go around your waist, remove the tape from the yarn at the top of the straws and discard the tape. Pull off the straws and discard them.

11. Carefully ease the woven part down the strands until it is in the center.

12. Using all strands of yarn at the ends, tie a knot in each one right up against the weaving to keep it from moving.

13. Repeat at the other end.

14. Beads or shells can be tied to the ends of the fringe if desired.

15. You can also divide the weaving by weaving only over and under the first three straws on either side for making different colored sections.

16. To add interest to your weaving, add new warp threads to the warp in the original weaving and thread straws on the new warp. *Weave* as before and, again, remove straws when the weaving is completed.

17. If you are making a person, different sections can be sewn together. Features can be woven in, or you may fashion them from cut pieces of yarn or felt and glue them on.

Level 1

Stuffed Butterflies is a lesson in creating larger than life, three-dimensional paper objects. It is an opportunity for students to think big, and to simply enjoy the unrestrictive nature of work done on a grand scale. In the next activity, *Planetary Achitecture,* students are asked to create a three-dimensional environmental landscape using a variety of found materials. Architecture is later introduced when students add appropriate structures to their newly created environments.

Stuffed Butterflies

Level 2

Point-to-Point Yarn Pictures is an activity that allows students to create interesting designs with yarn when they stretch it between nails which have been attached to a wooden base. *Soft Foam Masks* are created by cutting, arranging, and attaching colorful foam shapes together. *Constructional Problem Solving* presents the challenge of building a piece of sculpture using a wide variety of objects and forms. *Complete the Picture* is an activity that uses a magazine photo to spark the imagination and to serve as a starting point for a new composition.

Complete the Picture

Level 3

Wood Sculpture introduces assemblage techniques and also provides students with a new medium to explore. *Hand Puppets* introduce new puppetry techniques, including modeling with plastered gauze, increased characterization, and more elaborate costume design. *Aluminum Plaster Casting* introduces plaster as a media and casting as a process, as well as techniques for creating metal molds. *Metal Masks* further explores the mask as an art form as well as further exploring the techniques involved in tooling a metal surface.

Hand Puppets

Stuffed Butterflies

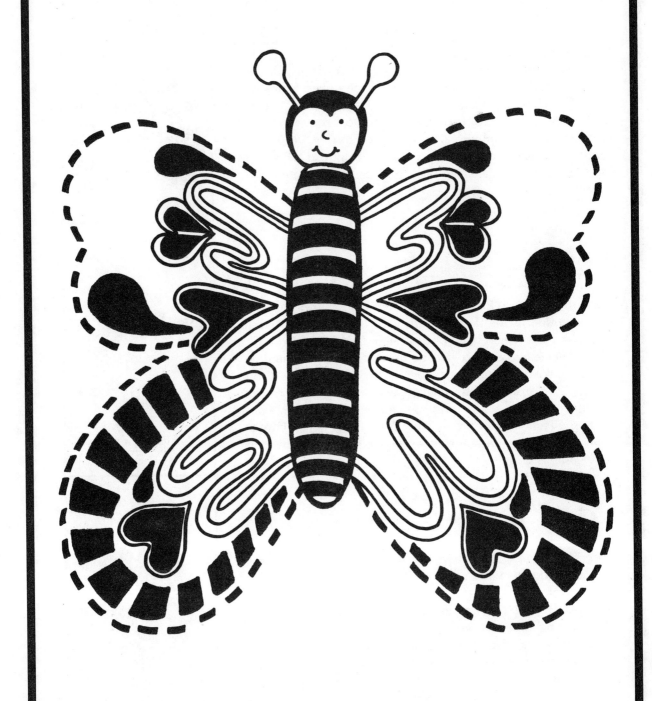

STUFFED BUTTERFLIES

Materials:

- pencil and eraser
- 2 large, heavy pieces of paper, 36″ × 48″
- newspaper
- tempera and brush
- stapler
- masking tape
- heavy string

Directions:

1. View slides or pictures of butterflies.
2. Draw a simple-shaped butterfly.
3. Include simple designs repeated on each wing.
4. Transfer the drawing to one 36″ × 48″ paper.
5. Paint in designs and paint the outline around the edge.
6. When dry, flip it over onto another piece of paper. Trace carefully around the drawing, which you should hold in place with masking tape. Cut the second butterfly drawing out and flip it over.
7. Draw identical butterfly designs on this side and paint.
8. When dry, put the two sides together with the painted side facing outward. Begin to staple the two sides together, but leave an opening about two feet long, which you should stuff lightly with crushed newspaper. Then, finish your stapling.
9. Holes can be punched in the top of each wing in order to hang the butterfly with heavy string.

Planetary Architecture

PLANETARY ARCHITECTURE

Materials:

- large cardboard box
- craft knife
- plaster impregnated gauze
- newspapers
- construction paper scraps
- glazed paper
- yarn
- silver glitter
- sand
- sawdust

- aluminum foil
- colored acetate
- styrofoam
- sugar cubes
- India ink
- chalk
- crayons
- tempera and brushes
- various glues

(Note: This is suggested as a group project.)

Directions:

1. You are a space explorer and have just landed for a rest on the uninhabited planet "Lambor." You need to have a shelter that will protect you from moondust but that will also allow you to look out and watch the sky as stars and spaceships whirl by and to observe the planet.

2. Carefully remove one side of your box and begin constructing your landscape by arranging crumpled mounds of newspaper in the bottom of the box. These newspaper hills and valleys should then be covered with overlapping layers of gauze. When dry, use paint to decorate the landscape. Other materials can be used as well; perhaps glitter for your mountain peaks, sand for your deserts, or sawdust for your canyons.

3. Next, using cardboard or styrofoam, design and construct your shelter. Attach this to your landscape with glue.

4. Preparations must be made for buildings for visitors to make them feel welcome, comfortable, and happy. See if any other buildings are necessary for the needs of the community.

5. Tape a piece of colored acetate across the opening in the box when you have finished building.

Point-to-Point
Yarn Designs

POINT-TO-POINT YARN DESIGNS

Materials:

- yarn
- scissors
- 3 to 5 pieces of wood of various lengths
- nails and hammer
- 1″ brads—small nails or staples for use with wood
- cardboard box
- straight pins
- liquid starch

Directions:

1. Take the lengths of wood and arrange a frame for the web, which will be irregular in shape. Nail them together by overlapping the edges.

2. Nail the brads onto the edge of this wood frame. These brads do not need to be evenly spaced. Hammer them about halfway in, so that the yarn can be fastened to the part sticking up. The irregularity of the shape of the frame and the uneven spacing of the brads help make an interesting design.

3. If a cardboard box is used, pins can be stuck to its edges.

4. Begin by tying the end of the yarn to one of the brads or pins.

5. Loop the yarn from one brad to another and from one side to another in what you consider to be an interesting design.

6. When finished, fasten the end of the yarn by wetting it with glue or liquid starch and pasting the end to another piece of yarn in the design.

7. Soak the completed yarn design in liquid starch.

8. When dry, remove the yarn design from the frame.

Soft Foam Masks

SOFT FOAM MASKS

Materials:

- foam carpet padding (purchase in rolls or collect scraps from a carpet company)
- heavy-duty scissors or snipes
- contact cement, white glue
- stapler
- string, yarn, fabric, and so forth

A **mask** is a decorative covering for the face. Masks have been used for thousands of years for a variety of purposes including: to prepare for hunting, for religious ceremonies, for superstitious healing, and for decoration. Today, we see masks on children at Halloween, masks painted on clowns' faces, on actors' faces, and so forth. In museums, we can see examples of American Indian, African, Eskimo, and theatrical masks. These masks are made of wood, clay, papier-mâché, and other materials.

Directions:

1. Masks may be used for fun and for decoration, such as Mardi Gras and Halloween and for more serious reasons, such as before a hunt or to ward off evil spirits from someone who is sick. Your mask will be just for fun.
2. Experiment by cutting, connecting, and forming various pieces of the foam.
3. Try twisting, layering, intertwining, and cutting through the foam sheets to achieve special effects.
4. When you think you have control of the foam, cut and form a head cover.
5. Once a comfortable cover or cap is achieved, develop features by cutting into the foam for eye holes, ears, nose, and mouth.
6. Add to the basic features in a manner that enhances the mask's decorative and expressive qualities.
7. Is your mask wearable? well crafted? expressive?

Constructional Problem Solving

CONSTRUCTIONAL PROBLEM SOLVING

Materials:

- balsa wood strips 1/16" thick
- sharp scissors
- cardboard
- block of styrofoam
- glue
- popsicle sticks
- egg carton cups
- paper straws

Directions:

Part I

1. Glue styrofoam to cardboad to form a base for the sculpture.
2. Cut out shapes in balsa wood.
3. Use large, medium, and small shapes.
4. Vary the shapes of each.
5. Try building up layers of balsa wood for a three-dimensional effect.
6. Glue some pieces and stick into the styrofoam base.
7. Let dry and paint.
8. Add to these pieces, designing higher and wider.
9. Turn the base around you as you work to be sure that it is interesting from all sides.

Part II

Do the same as above using egg carton cups.

Part III

Do the same as above using paper straws. (You have now experienced three construction problems including line, flat shapes, and three-dimensional shapes.)

Complete the Picture

COMPLETE THE PICTURE

Materials:

- 12″ × 18″ manila paper
- magazines
- scissors and paste or glue
- crayons or markers

Directions:

1. Cut out an object that is not a person or an animal from a magazine.
2. Glue it onto the manila paper.
3. Using your crayons or markers, complete an entire picture adding other objects, people, animals, or buildings to tell a story and to make your picture interesting to look at and out of the ordinary.

Wood Sculpture

WOOD SCULPTURE

Materials:

- small wood parts usually used for toys
- white glue or water soluble wood glue
- markers
- yarn, fabric
- popsicle sticks
- spools
- other small wood pieces
- 12″ × 18″ pieces of chipboard
- masking tape

Directions:

1. Look at the shapes of the wood and think about what can be made from them. Does one remind you of a headlight, a hat, a head, or a wheel?

2. Begin gluing various parts together. You might form cars, comic people, robots, airplanes, or furniture.

3. Think of an environment where your first object could be. Could it be an automobile race, a rock concert, a department store, or a place to eat?

4. Build more parts together to form other objects or people for your environment and glue them onto the chipboard.

5. Masking tape will hold stubborn pieces together until they dry.

6. Color may be added with markers.

7. Clothes and hair may be added with fabric and yarn.

8. The chipboard may also be colored with markers as part of the environment.

Hand Puppets

HAND PUPPETS

Materials:

- plaster-impregnated gauze
- old scissors
- warm water
- newspaper
- felt
- sharp scissors
- chalk
- yarn
- notions: rick-rack, lace, ribbon, buttons, and so forth
- tempera and brushes
- cotton
- fake fur
- masking tape
- oaktag
- gloss acrylic polymer

Directions:

1. Roll up a single sheet of newspaper into a round shape.
2. Roll this up inside another single sheet of newspaper. Squeeze into a good round shape and secure with masking tape.
3. Cut a piece of oaktag 3″ by 1″; roll it loosely around your "pointing" finger and secure with tape.
4. Tape this to the head to form the neck as shown.

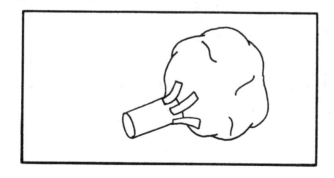

5. Tape on features for your puppet's face, which can be made by cutting oaktag shapes or squeezing or rolling a newspaper shape until it looks like the character you want to make. Exaggerate the size of all features.

6. You can add hats, chins, cheeks, ears, noses, mouths, teeth or whatever you like as shown.

7. Cut small pieces of gauze with your old scissors, dip in warm water, and begin to layer on your puppet's head, neck, and all the features, overlapping each piece for strength until you have completely covered your puppet.

8. Use your finger dipped in water to smooth out each piece and also to release the plaster to fill in the holes.

9. Let dry.

10. Paint with tempera, let dry, and coat with polymer.

11. Glue on yarn, raffia, or cotton if necessary.

12. Lay your hand on a piece of felt as shown.

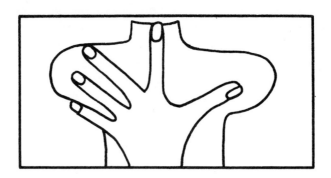

13. Use the chalk to trace around your hand in order to make a pattern for the costume as shown.

14. Cut this out, lay on another piece of felt, trace around your first felt pattern, and cut this out.

15. Use glue to fasten the two pieces together, leaving open the neck and bottom so that your hand can slip in.

16. Let dry.

17. Glue the neck inside the neck hole and tape until dry. Remove the tape.

18. Glue buttons, lace, fur, and so forth on the costume if desired.

Aluminum Plaster Casting

ALUMINUM PLASTER CASTING

Materials:

- pipe cleaner
- manila paper approximately 4″ × 6″
- newspaper
- aluminum tooling foil, 9″ × 12″
- pencils, tongue depressor

- plaster
- masking tape
- tempera paint
- sandpaper

Directions:

1. Begin by sketching your idea on a sheet of manila 4″ × 6″.

2. Next, fold masking tape around the edges of a 9″ × 12″ sheet of aluminum tooling foil. Then, center your drawing on top of the foil and secure it with a piece of tape.

3. Place a small stack of newspapers under the foil to act as a cushion.

4. Transfer your drawing from the manila paper to the foil by drawing over your outlines and remembering to press hard with your pencil.

5. When the transfer is complete, remove your drawing and begin embossing or tooling the foil by pushing some parts out and others in. This can be done with a dull pencil or tongue depressor. You can decorate and texturize the surface of the foil by using a sharper pencil and adding various patterns and markings.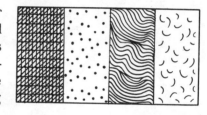

6. Next, use a ruler to outline four equal margins and cut along the lines indicated. Then fold up the corners and tape in place as shown.

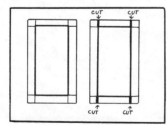 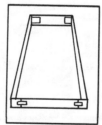

7. Now the plaster can be mixed and poured. While it is setting you may place a pipe cleaner shaped like this (see drawing on right) in the plaster. When your casting is dry this will serve as a hanger.

8. After removing the hardened plaster casting from the aluminum, you may wish to use sandpaper on any rough edges.

9. Now you are ready to complete your work by painting it.

Metal Masks

METAL MASKS

Materials:

- 9″ × 12″ paper
- 9″ × 12″ piece of aluminum foil
- pencil and eraser
- masking tape
- newspaper
- popsicle sticks and pencil-thin dowels cut to pencil length
- markers which will adhere to metal

Directions:

1. View slides or photos of masks made by American Indians and Eskimos.
2. Masks were used for religious and hunting ceremonies and for curing sickness, as well as for decoration.
3. Draw the outside shape of a face for your mask and include some type of ears.
4. Add unusually shaped eyes, nose, and mouth, keeping in mind whether you want to create a comedic or a frightening mask.
5. Add simple shapes to the forehead, cheeks, and chin.
6. Tape your drawing onto the 9″ × 12″ piece of foil and lay this on a pad of newspapers at least 2″ thick.
7. Trace over all the pencil lines by pressing hard enough with a pencil so that the lines are transferred to the foil.
8. Remove the drawing and begin to tool, or press down, inside the entire area of the nose using the popsicle sticks or dowels.
9. Flip the foil over and tool inside the entire area of the next space outward from the nose.
10. Flip over the foil and continue in the next area to tool so that the area is pressed out in one direction and the area next to it is tooled out in the opposite direction. (One area pops forward and the other area recedes.)
11. When all areas are tooled either forward or back, turn the side up where the nose "pops" forward and outline all shapes in black marker.
12. Fill in some of the shapes with markers of other colors so that you achieve a balance between the foil color and the marker colors.
13. The mask may be punched with holes at the top in order to hang it, or it may be stapled onto paper or cardboard for display.